Anonymous

The Soldier's Prayer Book

Anonymous

The Soldier's Prayer Book

ISBN/EAN: 9783337309268

Printed in Europe, USA, Canada, Australia, Japan

Cover: Foto ©Lupo / pixelio.de

More available books at **www.hansebooks.com**

THE

SOLDIER'S

PRAYER BOOK.

Lord, teach us how to pray as John taught his disciples.—LUKE xi, 1.

Likewise the Spirit also helpeth our infirmities: for we know not what we should pray for as we ought: but the Spirit itself maketh intercession for us with groanings which cannot be uttered.

And he that searcheth the hearts knoweth what *is* the mind of the Spirit, because he maketh intercession for the saints, according to *the will of G—*
Rom. viii, 26, 27.

CHARLESTON:
PUBLISHED BY THE SOUTH CAROLINA TRACT SOCIETY.
1863.

DEDICATION

This volume originated in the desire expressed by many soldiers to have forms of Prayer through which they might unite in social worship, and guide more perfectly their private devotions, and is now dedicated to GEORGE A. TRENHOLM, Esq., by whose approval and liberality it has been prepared and printed, and to A CAPTAIN IN THE ARMY, who has both encouraged its publication and will largely aid in its circulation.

CONTENTS.

I—SOCIAL PRAYERS—GENERAL.
  1. For the Sabbath.
  2. For any Occasion.
  3.   "   "
  4.   "   "
  5.   "   "

II—SOCIAL PRAYERS—SPECIAL.
  1. In anticipation of Battle.
  2. Prayer and Thanksgiving for Victory.
  3. After a Repulse or Defeat.
  4. For a Day of Thanksgiving.
  5. For a Day of Humiliation, Fasting, and Prayer.
  6. For the Revival of Religion.
  7. For our Rulers.
  8. For our Confederacy.
  9. For Absent Families.
  10. For Funeral Service.
  11. Against our enemies and for Peace.
  12. Thanksgiving for Peace.

III—PERSONAL AND PRIVATE PRAYERS.
  1. For a Professor of Religion.
  2. For a cold, careless Professor—a Backslider.
  3. Of a Sinner, for mercy, repentance, and faith.
  4. For a Sick or Wounded Soldier.
  5. On Recovery from Sickness.

IV—SHORT PRAYERS.
  1. For Morning.
  2. For Evening.
  3. On Going into Battle.

CONTENTS.

4. In Prospect of Battle.
5. On Sentinel and Picket Duty.
6. When Sick and Wounded.
7. For Divine Guidance.
8. A General Thanksgiving.
9. Thanksgiving.
10. General Prayer.
11. Collect.
12. Confession.
13. For Defence.
14. For Soldiers under Sentence of Death.
15. For Forgiveness.
16. For Direction.
17. On Deliverance from Enemies.
18. For those Exposed to Danger.
19. During our present National Troubles.
20. To be used in Ships of War.
21. Sailor's Prayer.
22. During a Storm.
23. Thanksgiving after a Storm.
24. For a Sick Person.
25. After Sudden Visitation.
26. For Close of any Service.
27. The Creed.
28. Gloria in Excelsis.
29. The Ten Commandments.

SELECTIONS OF SCRIPTURE.

1. For a Day of Thanksgiving.
2. For a Day of Humiliation.
3. For Victory.
4. For Repulse.
5. For Funerals.
6. For Peace.

SOCIAL PRAYERS.

GENERAL.

No. I.

For the Sabbath Day.

ALMIGHTY and most merciful God, Father, Son, and Holy Ghost, we thank thee for another Sabbath, which commemorates the finished works of creation and redemption. May we be enabled to rejoice and be glad in it, as the best of days, and the emblem and foretaste of that glorious rest which remains for the people of God. Though away from home, and far from the assemblies of thy people in our accustomed sanctuaries, may this Sabbath be made to each of our hearts a day of spiritual improvement, heavenly consolation, and near communion with thee, who art the Lord of the Sabbath. Separated from friends, and gathered together in this desert place, may we feel as did thy disciples when apart with thee in prayer. Be thou our Sanctuary. Make this solitary place a Bethel, none other than the house of God, and the very gate of Heaven. May our hearts be made to burn within us, and to exclaim, surely God is in this place, though we knew it not, to bless us, and to do us good.

Draw our hearts to thee. Draw them away from the vanities and vexations of this world. Excite within us spiritual hunger and thirst. Feed our souls with the bread of Heaven, and give us that living water, of which, if any man drink, he will never thirst any more. O satisfy us with thy mercy, so shall we rejoice, and be glad, all the days of our lives. May we find rest in thee from all sin, sorrow, and sadness.

Give us, O Lord, rest from our enemies who have come up against us, and wrongfully persecute and oppress us. Let no rude alarms of raging foes disturb our peaceful rest this day. Restrain their wrath, and make it to praise thee. But if compelled to fight, gird us with strength for battle, and enable us to contend earnestly for the faith once delivered to our fathers. Go up with us. Be thou the captain of our hosts, our leader, and commander. Help us and fight for us. O thou who art a God of Battles, and a man of war, with whom it is nothing to help, whether with many or with few, them that have no power, send us not up against this great multitude unless thou go up with us, for how will it be known that we are thy people unless thou go up with us. O God, who art our fathers' God, we rest on thee; and in thy name as a just God, and the avenger of the oppressed, we will go up against them. Let us not be dismayed or terrified because our enemies are lively and strong. Put them in fear, O God. Make them flee before us. Ride thou upon the whirlwind, and direct the storm of battle. May we live to praise thy great and glorious name, who hast gotten for us the victory, and triumphed gloriously.

With thy law and testimony before us, we appeal for the righteousness of our cause to thee, the Lord God omnipotent, who reignest with power supreme over all kingdoms and governments. Unto thee, O Lord, who didst give to our fathers, and to us by inheritance, this Southern land, and didst bring among us the heathen to be our servants, for good to them, and to the world, and for glory to thine own great name, unto thee do we now fly for protection from cruel and unjust men, who seek to disinherit and destroy us. Arise, O Lord, in thine anger. Plead thou our cause, and awake for us to the judgment thou hast commanded. Judge us, O Lord, and plead our cause against an ungodly, merciless, and perfidious nation, and grant that, being delivered from all connection with them, and dependent on thee alone, we may become a united and happy people, whose God is the Lord.

And now, O our Saviour, who didst on this day ascend far above all heavens, there to reign highly exalted above every name, until thou hast put all thine enemies under thy feet, come and reign in our hearts and minds. Set up within us thy kingdom of righteousness, and peace, and joy in the Holy Ghost. Restore peace to our bleeding land. Revive thy people who are scattered abroad everywhere. Reunite congregations and households. Restore commerce and agriculture, and may the earth again yield her increase, and the abundance of the sea bring prosperity. May our colleges again become the seminaries of learning, the fountains of wisdom, and the nurseries of pious and patriotic citizens, and of faithful and zealous ministers of the everlasting gospel; and may order, harmony, and peace be effectually and permanently restored, and truth and justice, religion and piety, universally prevail.

Hear us, O Christ, in these our prayers, which we offer unto God in thy name, and help us by the Holy Ghost, the Comforter, to call upon God, the Father, Son, and Holy Ghost, as thou hast taught, saying: Our Father, who art in heaven. Hallowed be thy name. Thy kingdom come. Thy will be done on earth, as it is in heaven. Give us this day our daily bread. And forgive us our trespasses as we forgive those who trespass against us. And lead us not into temptation, but deliver us from evil. For thine is the kingdom, and the power, and the glory for ever. Amen.

The grace of our Lord Jesus Christ, and the love of God our heavenly Father, and the fellowship of the Holy Ghost be with us all, now, henceforth, and for evermore. Amen.

No. II.

ALMIGHTY, everlasting, and ever blessed God, who for thine own glory made us of dust and breathed into our nostrils the breath of life, and didst illumine our minds with the inspiration of understanding, that we might serve thee always; permit us now to worship thee. We confess that we are sinners, and break thy laws every day in thought, word, and action. We confess that because of these sins we deserve to be cast into hell, and to endure thine anger for ever We confess that we are dead in sin, and cannot save ourselves from thy righteous condemnation and everlasting death, since no sorrow for sin can satisfy thy justice, and even our best works are so mixed with sin as to demand punishment. We thank thee, therefore, O most merciful God, that thou hast devised a way to save sinners, through Jesus, thine only begotten Son, the Saviour of mankind. We bless thee that Christ became a man, kept thy law, and died on the cross for us; that he rose again from the dead, and ever liveth at thy right hand, to plead for us in heaven; to give repentance and remission of sins; and to send the Holy Ghost, the Comforter, to convince, convert, and regenerate our hearts, and to help our infirmities by teaching us how to pray, to believe, and to repent, and by working in us to will and to do according to thy good pleasure. We bless thee that, when we could not obey thy law on account of sin, God, sending his own Son in the likeness of sinful flesh, and for sin, condemned sin in the flesh. We bless thee that salvation is thy GIFT, freely offered to all men; and that thy Holy Spirit, as a Spirit of wisdom, and of power, is bestowed upon all who ask it in sincerity.

Grant, O God, we beseech thee, that Holy Spirit unto us now, who are in circumstances of peculiar danger and temptation, to enable us to seek and to obtain the salvation of our souls; to accept thine offered mercy and thy gracious promises; to believe in Jesus Christ as set before us in thy glorious gospel; to come unto Him and find rest; so that we may take up our cross and follow Him, and never be ashamed to confess him before men, but may rather glory in his cross, and find his burden light, and his ways pleasantness and peace. Enable us to be frequent in prayer, and to offer up continually unto God the wishes of our hearts, casting all our cares and burdens upon thee, and ever looking unto Jesus, the author and finisher of our faith, for grace and mercy to help us according to our need.

Give us saving faith, inspiring hope, courageous confidence, and that love of Christ which will cast out all fear. Give us that true repentance which will make us forsake sin and dread to offend thee, our most merciful Father; or to dishonor Christ, our most blessed Lord and Saviour; or to grieve the Holy Spirit, our guide and guardian. Bestow upon us while living grace to prepare for dying, and for that judgment which is after death, that so, dying daily unto the world, our hearts may live in heaven, and rejoice in hope of the glory of God. Preserve us from the fear of man and from the power of our enemies. Prevent, if it be possible, the fierce conflict of battle, by making this war to cease, and causing even our enemies to be at peace with us. But if called ever to hazard our lives in bloody strife, teach our fingers to fight and our hands to war. Enable us to put on a manly courage. Imbue our minds with pure and lofty patriotism. Clothe us in the whole armor of God. Animate us with a holy boldness and self-sacrificing devotion, that we may contend earnestly and successfully for our wives, our mothers, and our sisters; for our homes and our sanctuaries; and for the blood-bought inheritance of civil and religious liberty bequeathed to us by our fathers. And grant that, if thou so ordainest, we may willingly die; whether we live or die, may we be the Lord's, so that to us to live may be Christ, and to die gain — even an entrance among the righteous who die to live; whose departing spirits are with Christ in paradise; and whose bodies shall come forth from the grave and ascend, with Christ, into heaven, to reign with him in glory through a blessed immortality.

And now, O God, our heavenly Father! as we deserve nothing of ourselves, we beseech thee to answer these our prayers for Christ's sake. Amen.

Our Father, who art in heaven, etc.*

The grace of our Lord Jesus Christ, etc.*

---

*Repeat as found in No. I.

No. III.

O GOD, who art a Spirit infinite, eternal, and unchangeable in thy being, wisdom, power, holiness, justice, goodness, and truth; we worship and adore thee. Thou art everywhere present. Thou art able to do whatsoever thou pleasest, and thou knowest all things. Our hearts are naked and open before thee, with all their sins and sorrows. Blessed be thy name, that while enthroned in majesty thou delightest in mercy; and that while thy glory is proclaimed by the heavens, and the earth, and all things thou hast made, thy tender mercies are over all thine other works.

We now approach thee as a God who is love; as the Lord God merciful and gracious; as the God and Father of our Lord and Saviour Jesus Christ; as in Christ reconciling sinners unto thyself; forgiving iniquity and blotting out transgression, and not willing that any should perish, but that all should come unto thee and find grace and mercy to help them. Enable us to draw nigh in faith, and with a holy boldness through Jesus Christ, who is the way, the truth, and the life; the Lamb of God, who taketh away the sins of the world, and who ever liveth, as our advocate with the Father, to make intercession for us.

O God, we are sinners before thee. We are guilty in thy sight. We are helpless and hopeless. We are without strength to save ourselves, and we are without excuse. We plead no merits of our own, for we have nothing of our own but our unbelief, ungodliness, and ingratitude toward Thee, in whom we live and move, and have our being. O God, wert thou to enter into judgment with us we could not stand in thy sight. But, O our justly offended Father, to whom can we go but unto thee? Thou alone canst save us, and pardon our sins, and justify us freely for Christ's sake. Our reliance is on thy mercy. Our confidence is in the Lord our Righteousness. Our hope is in thy word of invitation, promise, and forgiving love. Thou hast said, ask and ye shall receive, seek and ye shall find, knock and the door shall be opened. O Lord, behold us here asking, seeking, and knocking at the door of thy grace. May we now receive thy blessing, and find mercy, and feel as children at home in our Father's house, and in the enjoyment of thy pitiful compassion and loving kindness. Thou, O our Saviour, hast said, Come unto me all ye that are weary and heavy laden, and I will give you rest. Lord! through whom can we approach unto a holy and just God but by thee, for there is no other name under heaven by which we can be saved but thine only. O Lord our God! thou Saviour of the lost! thou Redeemer and friend of sinners, we now come to thee as a Prince and Saviour to give us repentance and remission of sins; to bestow upon us thy peace; to shed abroad in our hearts thy love; to impart to us the blessings of the gospel and the consolations of the Holy Ghost, that we may be filled with peace and joy in believing.

Come, O Saviour, near to us. Draw us nearer and nearer to thee. May we feel that thou art with us of a truth. May this camp be made to us a Bethel, none other than the house of God and the gate of heaven. Away from home, may we feel at home with thee who art the dwelling place of thy children. Separated from the loved and yearned for friends of earth, may we hold communion with them around thy mercy seat. Alone, solitary, and often sad, may we feel that we are, nevertheless, not alone, because thou, the beloved of our souls, art with us. Exposed to dangers, and to many hardships, and trials, and temptations, may we be supported by thy presence, sustained by thy power, and strengthened by thy might, so that we may feel—even in the state in which we now are—contented, cheerful, and happy. May our mutual intercourse be sweetened and sanctified, and may we enjoy much of the communion of saints, and the love of God, and the fellowship of the Holy Spirit in our seasons of private and social worship.

Preserve health where it is enjoyed. Restore it where it is enfeebled. Renew the vigor of those that have been wounded, so that they may run and not be weary, and walk and not faint. Comfort all who are sick and sorrowful. Bless our absent families and friends. Revive pure and undefiled religion in our churches, and pour out thy Spirit in a Pentecostal shower upon all our camps, until the voice of rejoicing and salvation shall be heard throughout our Southern land. Enable her soon to accomplish this warfare by the defeat of her enemies and the triumphant establishment of her independence, liberty, and peace. Remove from us, O Lord, this war which is thy sword. Put up thy sword into thy scabbard and ordain peace for us, for thou art the God of peace, who hast proclaimed peace on earth and good will to men. Grant these requests, thou Prince of peace, and to thee, with the Father, and the Holy Ghost, we will render all praise, thanksgiving, and glory, now, henceforth, and for ever. Amen.

Our Father, who art in heaven, etc.

The grace of our Lord Jesus Christ, etc.

No. IV

O GOD, who art the inspirer and hearer of prayer, teach us now to pray in an acceptable time in which we may be heard, and with the effectual, fervent prayer of the righteous, which availeth much. As thou hast given us an opportunity with one accord to make our common supplication unto thee, so give us hearts to pray. May the Holy Spirit help our infirmities, for we know not how to pray, nor what we should pray for as we ought. O holy and blessed Comforter! make intercession for us, with groanings that cannot be uttered. And, seeing we have not a High Priest who cannot be touched with a feeling of our infirmities, but one who was in all respects tempted like as we are, yet without sin, enable us to come with boldness unto the throne of grace, that we may obtain mercy, and find grace to help in time of need. And oh, do thou, who in the days of thy flesh didst offer up prayers and supplications with strong crying and tears unto Him that was able to save from death, hear now our prayer. Intercede for us, and become thyself the author of eternal salvation unto each of our souls.

We are now in the flesh. We groan under the bondage of its corruption, the lusts of the eyes, the lusts of the flesh, and the pride of life. The law in our members wars against the law of our God, so that when we would do good, evil is present with us. Give us, O Saviour, power to mortify our bodies, and keep them under, and to crucify the flesh with its affections and lusts, that we may enjoy the liberty of the children of God, and present unto thee body, soul, and spirit, as a living sacrifice which is our only reasonable service.

We, Lord, are now, even as thou also once wert, in the wilderness, tempted of the Devil, compassed about with manifold trials, exposed to innumerable dangers, and encircled by malignant enemies, who wrongfully come up against us and seek to destroy us. O holy and sympathizing Saviour, permit us to lean upon thee as our Beloved. Keep us by thy power. Open up for us in this dreary desert a fountain of living water and wells of salvation, and lead us, as pilgrims and strangers, in the right way to that inheritance which is incorruptible and undefiled, and cannot fade away. Be thou our guide and guardian. Keep us near thy side. Uphold us by thy powerful hand. Strengthen us in our weakness. Comfort us in all our tribulations. Defend and deliver us. Subdue our enemies under us. Give us valor and victory. Cause this war to cease. Make our enemies to be at peace with us. Compel their wrath to praise thee, and the remainder thereof restrain. Perform toward us the mercy shown to our fathers, and remember thy holy covenant with them, that we, being saved from our enemies, and from the hand of all that hate us, may serve thee, without fear, in holiness and righteousness before thee, all the days of our life.

Let no trial come upon us but what thou, O our compassionate Saviour, wilt enable us to bear. Send forth ministering spirits to minister to our necessities, to succor us, and to encamp around about us and deliver us. Preserve the lives and health of our officers and soldiers. Give to our officers wisdom, skill, and power, that they may lead us in a plain and safe path because of our enemies. Put thy Spirit within them, and grant them thy salvation. Make them counsellors as well as commanders, that they may combine wisdom and sympathy with authority and strict discipline, and may thus secure the devotion as well as the obedience of their troops. Imbue the heart of every soldier with the spirit of implicit and cheerful obedience. May they endure all their hardships, and discharge every duty, as imposed by God; and do thou, O merciful Father, give them patience and resignation to thy will, and a single eye to thy glory, and to the honor and happiness of their country. Grant them a speedy release from the toils and trials of soldier life. Restore them soon to their homes, and may they live long to enjoy the abundant blessings of peace and prosperity. Comfort all among them that mourn. Awaken, convince, and convert the impenitent. Guide the weary, seeking sinner to the Saviour, and grant him peace and joy in believing. Increase the faith and piety of thy true disciples. Heal and restore the backsliding, and love us all freely. Prepare us while living for dying, and when dying for death, so that dying may be going home, a welcome discharge, and a joyful entrance into thine everlasting kingdom.

Hear and answer these petitions, O God, for the sake of Jesus Christ, our blessed Saviour and Redeemer, to whom, with the Father and the eternal Spirit, be everlasting praises. Amen.

Our Father, who art in heaven, etc.

The grace of our Lord Jesus Christ, etc.

No. V.

ALMIGHTY God, fountain of life and immortality, source of every blessing, the gracious Redeemer of our souls, we praise and magnify thy glorious name for the gift of thy only Son, for the inspiration of the Holy Comforter, and for the blessed hope of everlasting life. We thank thee, adorable Redeemer, that thou didst so love the world as to pour out thy precious blood for sinful man, and that this day thy gracious intercession prolongs our life and secures the innumerable blessings we continually receive. Would it please thee to pardon the sins we have committed against thee, for we have violated thy law; we have grieved thy Spirit; we have followed the desires of an evil heart; we have yielded to temptations and lust, and pride and anger; we have sinned against thee with our lips and in our hearts through all our life. O most merciful Saviour, forgive our transgressions. Bring us not into judgment. Banish us not from thy presence, but in thy infinite compassion renew and sanctify our hearts. Wash us in thy blood. Anoint us with thy Spirit. Unfold thy character and law to our minds. Teach us to do thy holy will. And so subdue and destroy all worldly passions and evil habits that we may adoringly love thee and possess the mind that was in Christ Jesus our Lord. O Spirit of all grace and comfort, quicken our conscience, grant to us the evidence and witness of acceptance, and create within us the holy purpose of consecrating ourselves unreservedly to the glory of God, and so guide us that we may live a useful and happy life in Christ Jesus our Saviour.

Almighty God, we commit us to thy care.

Guard us in danger. Preserve us from disease, and in the day of battle cover our heads. Deliver us, we beseech thee, from ambitious, and revengeful, and blood-thirsty passions, and animate us with a holy love of country and respect for our officers, and give to us that unity of purpose and power, and so display thy providence that our enemies may be smitten, and the lustre of a great victory gather around the brow of the Son of God. Save our country and our rulers, keep our people in union of spirit and dependence on Thee, and make thy law the great pillar of government.

O Father of mercy, bless our homes, fold to thy guardian bosom those whom we have left, and console and preserve them with thy most tender care, should any of us be called to die. Deliver us from the temptations and depravity of the camp, and grant that in thy good providence we may return to our homes to love thee with a perfect heart, and to serve thee with a willing mind. In every moment of darkness and fear, of weakness and want, in camp or in hospital, on the march or in battle, come thou near, O Son of God; be thou our shield, and song, and the great Rock of our defence.

GENERAL.

O Father of mercy, our life, our souls, our immortality are in thy hands. Increase within us a lively faith in thy mercy through Christ Jesus, and in thy all-protecting providence, that whatever our condition may be, in sickness or in health, in life or in death, we may find acceptance through his precious blood, and enjoy the blessed hope of everlasting life.

O Lord, we would cheerfully submit to our duties, dangers, and difficulties, with an humble reliance on thy fatherly care. Strengthen our purpose, and confirm us in a determined resistance to every sin, and assist us in the regular and faithful discharge of every religious and civil duty. Hear us, we beseech thee, O Merciful Father, and accept us in Jesus Christ who died for us; and to thee, the God of all grace, we will ascribe praise and glory for ever and ever, through the infinite love of Christ Jesus our Lord. Amen.

Our Father, who art in heaven, etc.

The grace of our Lord Jesus Christ, etc.

SPECIAL.

No. I.

A Prayer in anticipation of Battle.

O GOD, Father, Son, and Holy Ghost, thou hast said, Call upon me in the day of trouble, and I will hear thee and deliver thee. We, therefore, now approach thee in our time of danger. The enemy is near and round about us, and we may soon be called upon to hazard our lives in the field of battle; and some of us be wounded or suddenly cut down in the midst of our days. O God, who hast called thyself a man of war, be not far from us. Thou didst fight for Israel; and our fathers have told us what wonders thou didst perform in their days; how thou didst dash in pieces their enemies, and subdue them under them; and how in the greatness of thine excellency thou didst overthrow those that rose up against them. We, therefore, look to thee who didst deliver them from death, and beseech thee to go with our army; to become our Leader and Commander; and to teach our hands to war, and our fingers to fight, that we may wax valiant, and fight manfully, and be made mighty through Thee, to drive back and to destroy our enemies.

We thank and praise Thy glorious Name, that thou hast afflicted us less than our iniquities deserved. Remember not against us our innumerable offences. Let thy tender mercies save us from their guilt, and wash us from their pollution in the fountain opened for sin and uncleanness. O Lord, be gracious unto us for Christ's sake, that being justified by faith in him we may have peace with God, and with our own consciences. Impart to us a sweet hope that thou art our reconciled God and Father; that the spirit of love may cast out all fear. Hearken unto our voice, O Lord, while we now cry unto thee. Have mercy upon us, and hear us. Be thou, O Lord, the strength of each heart, our light, and our salvation; and then, though an host should come up against us, yet shall we not be afraid of them who, when they have killed the body, have nothing more that they can do.

But, while thus confessing our sins, and imploring mercy for Christ's sake, we plead before thee the righteousness of our cause. We contend for liberty of conscience, liberty of worship, and liberty of life. We stand in defence of home, and happiness, and the heritage thou hast given us, and which our fathers bought for us with their own blood. Arise, O thou to whom belongeth vengeance, and plead our cause against an unjust and ungodly nation, who have wrongfully come up against us to destroy us.

O most powerful and glorious Lord God, who sittest in the throne judging right: we beseech thee to take the cause into thine own hand, and judge between us and our enemies. Stir up thy strength, O Lord, and come and help us, and avenge us speedily for the oppression of the poor; for the sighing of the needy; for the miseries of the widow and the orphan; for thy sanctuaries defiled; for thy Name blasphemed; for thy laws despised and made subject to a higher law; for virtuous chastity dishonored, and innocent blood shed without cause; for thousands of thine own dear children — the friends of Jesus, and the nursing fathers of thy Church — ruthlessly slaughtered; for these things, O God, who wilt not hold their perpetrators guiltless, arise and be known by the judgments thou shalt execute upon them. And may it be made evident to us, and to our enemies, that this battle is the

Lord's, that the Lord God of hosts is on our side, and fighteth for us, and that thou art our Saviour and mighty deliverer.

We have no might, O Lord, against this great company who come up against us, neither know we what to do, but our eyes are upon thee. Lord, it is nothing with thee to help with many, or with them that have no power, for the battle is not to the strong, neither is it by might nor by power. With thee, O Lord, is wisdom and strength. Thou hast power to exalt, and to cast down. Thine, O Lord, is the greatness and the victory. O Lord our God, go with us, and lead us up against our enemies, and save us. Inspire our generals with wisdom, and power, and strategy, and skill, and cover their heads in the hour of battle, and let no weapon aimed against them prosper. Imbue the minds of all our officers and soldiers with confidence in thee, and in each other; with calmness, coolness, valor, and heroic devotion; and crown our contest with victory.

And now, O God our Saviour, into thy hands we commit each other, not knowing what shall befall us; but being joyfully assured that with thee are the issues of life and death; that thou hast the keys of death and the grave; and that as thou appointest for each one of us the time, and place, and manner of our death, thou art able to keep all that we now cast upon thy merciful providence, so that if we live we may live unto the Lord, and if we die we may die unto the Lord, that whether living or dying we may be the Lord's.

Our Father, who art in heaven, etc.

The grace of our Lord and Saviour, etc.

No. II.

A Prayer and Thanksgiving for Victory.

ALMIGHTY, everlasting, and ever blessed God, who is a God, like unto thee, glorious in holiness, fearful in praises, a God who doest wonders? Thou rulest the raging of the sea and the tumult of the people; when the waves thereof arise thou stillest them. Thou hast discomfited and driven back for us the gathered hosts of our enemies. Thou hast scattered them with thy strong arm. The stout hearted are broken in pieces as a potter's vessel. At thy rebuke, O God, they fled, and the chief captains and the mighty men of valor have slept their last sleep. This is the Lord's doing, and it is marvellous in our eyes. We would now stand still, and see the salvation of God. With wonder, gratitude, and praise we exclaim, what hath God wrought! Not unto us, O God, not unto us, but unto thy great name, be all the glory. Thine own right hand and thy holy arm have gotten us this victory.

We bless thee, O God, for our able generals, gallant officers, and heroic soldiers. But it has not been by the skill of our generals, nor by the intrepidity of our officers, nor by the multitude of our mighty men of valor we have been saved. If it had not been that thou, O Lord, wast on our side to fight for us, and to break the bow, the shield, the sword, and the battle, we may now well say that when the hosts of our enemies rose up against us and compassed us about like bees, then had they swallowed us up quick, when their wrath against us was kindled; then the waters had overwhelmed us, the stream had gone over our souls. Blessed be the Lord, who has not given us as a prey unto their teeth. Our soul is escaped as a bird out of the snare of the fowler. The snare is broken, and we are escaped. Our help was in thy name, O Lord, who made heaven and earth. Praise waiteth for thee, O God, in Zion. We would think of thy loving kindness in the midst of thy temple. Safety cometh from thee, O Lord. Thou wast our shield and buckler. Thou, O Lord, didst preserve us from fear, so that we were not terrified because of them. Thou didst turn the perilous edge of battle, riding upon its whirlwind, and directing its storm. Thou hast broken forth upon our enemies as a breach of waters. Thou hast avenged us, and brought the people under us. May all thy people know that this battle was the Lord's, who has given it into our hands, for thou, O God, hast power to help and to cast down. Blessed be the Lord, who has had mercy upon us, and saved us, not by sword, nor by battle, nor by horses, nor by horsemen; but by the Lord, our God, who has done marvellous things. Thine, O Lord, be the greatness, and the power, and the glory, and the victory, and the majesty. We thank thee, and praise thy glorious Name.

But oh, our good and gracious God, thou hast also called us to a deep humiliation and sorrow, by turning our victory into mourning for the many brave and good men through whose heroic deaths Thou hast given it to us. We would thank thee for all in them that was lofty and honorable in character and conduct; for that self-sacrificing devotion which made them fearless of danger, faithful unto death, and willing, by their deaths, to secure the independence and glory of their country. We thank thee for the noble example of their lives, and their illustrious testimony to the righteousness of our cause, which they have sealed with their blood. May their names be held in everlasting remembrance by a grateful country, and grace with honor their remotest posterity. Sustain the hearts of their bereaved widows and orphans, and provide for, protect, and bless them through life, and in death.

Let thy merciful compassions, O Lord God, be extended to our wounded comrades. Sustain them in the endurance of their agonizing pains of body and affliction of soul. Inspire them with patient resignation to thy holy will, and impart to them the consolations of thy gracious presence. May they rejoice in being counted worthy to suffer in a cause so sacred and lofty. May their spared lives lead them to repentance and reconciliation with thee, through Jesus

Christ our Lord; and may they yet live to do battle for their endangered country, and to enjoy the rewards of a peaceful and prosperous future, and the blissful hope of everlasting life.

Take under thy most tender and compassionate care those whose wounds are mortal, and whom thou hast appointed to die. Disarm death of its sting, and the grave of its victory. In the midst of their torturing pain, and sinking spirits, and dying strife, may Thy consolations delight their souls. Visit them with thy salvation. Oh, holy Saviour, give them thy peace. Send them thy blessed Comforter. Make thy grace sufficient for them. Lift their hearts to thee, and to heavenly joys. Deliver them from all fears and doubts. Sustain and cheer them when entering into the dark valley of the shadow of death. Give them victory beyond the grave, and a crown of glory that fadeth not away.

And now unto God's gracious mercy and protection we commit ourselves. The Lord bless us, and keep us. The Lord make his face to shine upon us, and be gracious unto us. The Lord lift up his countenance upon us, and give us peace both now and for evermore. Amen. To thee, therefore, our dear Father, our Creator, Protector, Governor, and Defender, and to thy beloved Son Jesus Christ, our only Prince, Redeemer, Justifier, and Intercessor, and to thy Holy Spirit, our Sanctifier, Instructor, and Comforter, be all dominion, power, and glory, for ever and ever. Amen.

Our Father, who art in heaven, etc.

The grace of our Lord Jesus Christ, etc.

No. III.

Prayer and Confession after a Repulse or Defeat.

ALMIGHTY and most merciful God, our Heavenly Father, the protector of all who put their trust in thee, and the refuge of all who fly unto thee, and a very present help in time of need to all who call upon thee, thou seest us prostrate in thy presence to do homage to thy supreme majesty; to confess our sins to thee, and to cast upon thee our burden of grief. Did we follow the present emotions of our own hearts, we would not presume to approach thee, but would fly from thy presence. But, O Lord, though our sins and miseries oppress us, thy mercies lift us up. We lay hold of thy sweet and soothing promises, which are all yea and amen in Christ Jesus, and secured to us by thine immutable covenant and unchangeable perfections. Thou art a God merciful and gracious, slow to anger, and abundant in goodness; forgiving sin and imputing not iniquity, compassionately receiving thy backsliding children who return unto thee with penitent and contrite hearts, and exercising toward them yearning sympathy, even when thou chastenest them for their good. Encouraged by such merciful assurances, our trembling hearts, full of fears and cast down and disquieted within us, are inspired with ardent hopes that thou wilt grant us the present aid of thy powerful providence and illimitable grace.

We have *always*, O Lord, need of thy comforting, sustaining, and directing presence; but now we are in circumstances of such deep calamity and distress that thou alone canst direct and defend us. Thou hast put us to shame before our enemies. Thou hast deeply humbled our pride, and disappointed our hopes, and mortified our ambition. Thou hast not gone up with our armies. We thought, O Lord, thou wert with us as at other times, and knew not that the Lord had departed from us. But thou hast discomfited us before the enemy, and turned us back, and smitten us. We acknowledge, O Lord, thy holy, wise, and powerful providence in our calamity. *Thou* hast brought this evil upon us, and it is by thee we have been stricken and afflicted. For all things come alike from thee, and thou hast taught us that no affliction springeth from the dust, neither cometh by chance, and that there can be no evil in a city which thou hast not done.

Thou, O Lord, hast brought this evil upon us because we have sinned against thee and provoked thee to enter into judgment with us. Father, we have sinned against heaven and in thy sight. Our own hearts condemn us, and thou, O Lord, art greater than our hearts, and knowest all things. Our daily lives, and words, and actions testify against us and condemn us. We have sinned with our lips, and our tongues have uttered ungodly speeches against thee. Out of our hearts have proceeded evil thoughts, fornication, adultery, and impurity. We are selfish, sensual, and unholy. Pride has compassed us about as with a chain. We have uttered great swelling words of vanity, saying, who is the Lord that he should reign over us. We have lived as if we were our own, and not as those who have been created, and redeemed by thee. We have forsaken and forgotten thee, and lived without God and without hope in the world. We have set at naught thy word and commandments, neglected thy great salvation, left unread thy holy book, dishonored thy holy Sabbaths, profaned thy divine and awful name, trifled with the salvation of our souls, refused to hear, to obey, and to believe upon thy Son, our blessed Lord and Saviour, and have withheld from him our hearts, and the open confession of our mouths, and the living sacrifice of obedient lives. We have grieved the Holy Spirit of promise, and resisted all his gracious influences working in us to will and do of thy good pleasure. We have trusted in our own wisdom, and might, and bravery, and boasted of our skill and superiority, and glorified in our leaders and armies, and have said that by our own hands we have gotten us our victories. We have forgotten, O God, thy manifold mercies in the preservation of our lives, the healing of our diseases, the deliverances of our armies, and defeats of our enemies, in the supply of our daily wants, and the protection thrown around our generals, officers, and soldiers amid the diseases of the camp and the dangers of battle. We have murmured and complained against thee on account of our trials, and forgotten all thy benefits with which thou hast daily enriched us. We have restrained prayer before God, and have not called upon thee in sincerity and truth, but have mocked thee with *words* of prayer, while our hearts were far from thee. For these, and innumerable other sins with which we and our people have sinned against thee, O God, thou hast righteously entered into judgment with us, and mightest justly cast us off for ever and give us up as a prey to our enemies.

But, O merciful God and Saviour, though we have thus grievously provoked thee to anger and moved thee to jealousy, be not very wroth with us, and retain not thine anger against us. Pardon our iniquities, for thy Name's sake, for they are great. Reconcile us unto thyself through Christ our Saviour, that we may have peace with thee. Forsake not thy sanctuaries, and forget not thy covenant. Give not our glory to our enemies, even the inheritance which thy right hand purchased, which thou didst give to our fathers after driving out the heathen before them, and in which thou didst make them to dwell safely, so that they feared not. Return, therefore, O Lord, and let it repent thee concerning thy servants. O remember not against us former iniquities, but let thy tender mercies speedily restore us, for we are brought very low. Help us, O Lord, for the glory of thy name, and turn us, O God of our salvation, and cause thine anger toward us to cease. Forgive the iniquity of our people, and cover all their sins. Revive us again, that thy people may rejoice.

God of our fathers, and God of battles, hear these warriors who now call upon thee. Answer us from thy secret place of thunder. Keep not silence, O God. Hold not thy peace. Our enemies, with one consent, have taken crafty counsel against thy people and are confederate against them, saying, Come, let us cut them off from being a nation, that the name of the Confederate States may be no more in remembrance. O God, in whom, though thou slayest us, we will still trust, thou standest in the congregation of the mighty and judgest among them who think they are gods. Arise, O God, and judge them, that they may know that Thou whose name alone is Jehovah art the most high over all the earth. Be thou known among them and in our sight, by revenging the blood of thy servants which they have shed like water. Pour out upon them thy wrath, for they have devoured our substance, and laid waste our dwelling places, and burned thy churches, and ravaged our cities, and outraged our women, and blasphemously set at naught all laws, human and divine. O thou Supreme Judge and Ruler of the earth, let these crimes, and the cries of mothers, wives, and daughters, and of helpless widows and orphans come up before thee, and do thou avenge us speedily. Defend the poor and fatherless. Do justice to the afflicted and needy. Let the sighing of the prisoner come before thee. According to the greatness of thy power and mercy preserve thou those that are appointed to die. Render unto our enemies sevenfold into their own bosom. Persecute them with thy tempest, and make them afraid with thy storm, and may the angel of death destroy them. Fill their faces with shame, that they may seek thy name, O Lord, and repent and be saved, lest they be confounded and troubled for ever, and perish with all thine enemies, O Lord.

Quicken Thou us, so will not we go back from thee, and we will call upon thy name. Turn us again, O Lord of hosts, and cause thy face to shine upon us, and give us strength for battle and confidence, because of thy presence with us, and approval of us and of our righteous cause, and we shall yet be saved.

So we, thy people, and sheep of thy pasture, will give thee thanks for ever. We will show forth thy praise to all generations.

Our Father, who art in heaven, etc.

The grace of our Lord Jesus Christ, etc.

No. IV.

For a Day of Thanksgiving.

THINE, O Lord, is the greatness, and the power, and the glory, and the victory, and the majesty, for all that is in the heaven and the earth is thine. Both riches and honor come of thee, and thou reignest over all, and in thine hand are power and might, and in thine hand it is to make great, and

to give strength unto all. Thou, O Lord,
art our Father and our Redeemer. We
thank thee, and praise thy glorious name,
which is exalted above all blessing and
power. O God, thou art our God, and we
will praise thee, our fathers' God, and we
will exalt thee.

Blessed be thy great and glorious name
who hast done so great things for us, whereof we are glad. We rejoice in thy judgments, O God. We come into thy presence
with thanksgiving, and make a joyful noise
unto thee with psalms. We are thankful
unto thee, and bless thy name. Thou, O
Lord, art our rock, and our fortress, and our
deliverer. When the pains of death compassed us and the floods of ungodly men
made us afraid, in our distress we called upon
thee, and thou didst hear our voice out of
thy temple. Thou didst send from heaven
and draw us out of many waters, from the
power of our strong enemies and from them
that hated us. Thou hast girded us with
strength to battle, and hast subdued under us
them that rose up against us, and broken
their bands asunder. Let the heavens rejoice and let the earth be glad, and let men
say the Lord reigneth. Unto thee, O Lord,

we would give the glory due unto thy name. We would bring an offering, and worship and bow down before thee in the beauty of thine holiness.

How wonderful have been thy works toward us as a people, O Lord. Truly may it be said of us that as a nation we were born in a day. Thou hast not done such great things for any people under the whole heavens as thou hast done for us. We adore thy holy, wise, and powerful providence, which for so many years, and in such inscrutable ways, has led to the division of this great country, so as to sever us from a Union which was in its origin unnatural and impolitic, and in its experience disastrous to every object contemplated by it, and to every interest of these Southern states, and perverted to sectional injustice, usurpation, and tyranny, and to a fanatical and irrepressible conflict with the institutions, property, peace, and good name of the South. We adore, O God, that mighty, though invisible power by which thou didst infatuate our enemies to prosecute this war against us; which united the people of our Southern states with such marvellous harmony, under a constitution recognizing Thy supremacy, and framed with humble prayer for thy guidance, and in confident reliance upon thy protecting care; which has preserved us from all discord and division; which has crowned our arms with such illustrious victories; which has sustained and encouraged us in times of disaster, and under all the inhumanities of our merciless foes; which has crowned the year with thy goodness, and supplied the necessities of man and beast; which has given us fame and favor among the nations; which has preserved our slaves in loyalty and industrious quietness; which has made us mighty to resist the utmost power and gigantic resources of our enemies; which has more and more melted us a people into one concentrated mass of living valor and patriotic endurance, while our enemies have been divided and distracted; and which is now inspiring us with the assurance of success, and the animating hope of a peaceful, propitious, and honorable independence. We would in a special manner thank thee, O Father of mercies, for those recent events, etc. [*Here enumerate.*]

And now, O Lord, our good and gracious God, continue with us. Abide among us. Go up with us and with our armies, and fight for us, that all may know that thou art with us; that this battle is the Lord's, and that our cause is of God, and must prevail. Strengthen, therefore, the things which thou hast already wrought for us and by us. Give ear, O Shepherd of Israel; thou that dwellest between the cherubim, shine forth. Stir up thy strength, and come and save us. O Lord, our God, how long wilt thou be angry against the prayer of thy people. Turn us again, O God of Hosts, and cause thy face to shine and we shall be saved.

We bless thee, O Lord, who dividest the nations their inheritance, and settest the bounds of the people, that thou hast planted us in a very fruitful field, and hast not made the wilderness our habitation, nor the barren land our dwelling. Lord, thou hast dealt favorably with our land, and made it to yield its increase and bring forth abundantly, both for the clothing and the food of man. Thou hast given us a pleasant land—Emmanuel's land. Thou hast set up thy tabernacle among us, and thy sanctuaries are in the midst of us, and because thou hast loved our people, therefore thou hast set a good government over us: to insure domestic tranquillity and provide for the common defence; to promote the general welfare and secure the blessings of liberty to ourselves and our posterity. We have heard, O Lord, with our ears, and our fathers have told us what thou didst for them in their days; and as we have heard, so have we seen their glory made to appear unto their children. And now, as we think of all thy loving kindness in the midst of thy temple, let our thanksgiving and prayer come up with acceptance before thee. May thy answer in our hearts cheer us, and thy presence embolden, and thy providence uplift us. Fill our hearts with the glow of living patriotism, and nerve them with fortitude and valor in enduring, daring, and doing all that is needful to successful resistance and to triumphant peace. Establish thou the work of our hands; yea, the work of our hands establish thou it.

Based upon justice, truth, and equity, imbued with the spirit of honor, good will, and magnanimity, and guided by thy word, will, and providence, may our country be exalted more and more in name and in honor among the nations of the earth, and established as a holy people unto thyself. May she be blessed by thee in the city and in the field;

in the fruit of her body and the fruit of her ground; in the fruit of her cattle, increase of kine, and flocks of sheep; in her basket and in her store; in her agriculture, her commerce, and her manufactures; in science, learning, and piety; in statesmanship and public faith.

Let the wickedness of the wicked come to an end, but establish thou the just, O righteous God. Inspire many to stand up for thee against the workers of iniquity, and for the truth, purity, and power of thy glorious gospel. Counsel our counsellors, and give our senators wisdom, that the things which belong to a nation's peace and prosperity may not be hid from a nation's counsels. May our rulers be just, ruling in the fear of God. May our judges remember that they judge not for men but for the Lord, who is with them in judgment, that the fear of the Lord may be upon them. Make all in authority over us able men, men of truth, fearing God and hating covetousness, that they may defend the poor and fatherless, do justice to the afflicted and needy, and vindicate the oppressed.

Bless, O Lord, our soldiers who jeopard their lives in the high places of the field.

Give them the shield of thy salvation. Let thy right hand hold them up, and cover their heads in the day of battle. Through thee may they do valiantly. Yea, let God himself tread down our enemies. As they have taken the sword let them perish by the sword. Give them as dust to our sword, and as stubble to our bow. Let us be a people saved by the Lord, as the shield of our help and the sword of our excellency; and make our enemies sensible that the Lord of Hosts is with us, and fighteth for us against them.

Preserve the life and health of our President and generals, for whom we thank thee, and for whom we supplicate thy continued blessing; that, endued with all wisdom, skill, and power, they may become our deliverers. Give unity, efficiency, and all needful grace and guidance to our officers, and the spirit of obedience, alacrity, and devotion to our soldiers. Keep them in good health, heart, and hope, and comfort them under all their hardships. Restore the strength of the wounded and sick. Prepare the living for dying, and the dying for the death of the righteous, and recompense them all for their heroic sacrifices and sufferings, with thy favor and the everlasting gratitude of their redeemed and regenerated country.

Pitifully compassionate the misery of them that are in captivity. Let the sighing of the prisoner come before thee. Give them grace, though bound in affliction and iron, to cry unto thee in their trouble, and to humble themselves, and pray, and seek thy face, so that even in the innermost prison they may sing praises unto God. Be with them as with Joseph, and show them mercy, and grant them thy salvation. Strengthen their faith and patience in suffering, that they may both hope and quietly wait until thou shalt open their prison doors, and set them in safety into a large place.

May the time speedily come when our enemies shall be at peace with us; when thou wilt break the bow, and the sword, and the battle; when thy people shall be no more terrified by rude alarms of raging foes; when thou wilt make this war to cease, and ordain peace for us; and our people shall learn war no more. O Thou that savest by thy right hand them that put their trust in thee from those that rise up against them, show us thy marvellous loving kindness, and hide us under the shadow of thy wings.

Thou who hast delivered—doth deliver—we trust and pray, wilt yet deliver us from all our fears, that we may dwell safely under our own vine and fig tree, none daring to make us afraid.

The God of peace accept our thanks, and hear our prayers, and grant unto us the things we have requested of him, and cause his face to shine upon us for the Lord's sake, who is the son of his love; and unto God, Father, Son, and Holy Ghost be glory as it was in the beginning, is now, and ever shall be, world without end. Amen.

Our Father, who art in heaven, etc.

The grace of our Lord Jesus Christ, etc.

No. V.

For a Day of Humiliation, Fasting, and Prayer.

ALMIGHTY and most merciful God, who art the Rock of our Salvation, our refuge and defence, the hope of Israel and the Saviour thereof in the time of trouble, regard in tender compassion the supplications of thy servants who now approach thee in the name of thy dear Son, Jesus Christ our Lord. In unison with thy people throughout our land, we now humbly approach thee, the great and terrible God, to whom belongeth vengeance. Thy judgments are abroad among us. We are brought very low. The whole land mourneth because of the oppressions of the enemy. Our cities are destroyed, our sanctuaries are desolate, our homes are ravaged, and our fields laid waste. Our people are scattered and peeled, suffering the loss of all things, and enduring persecution, privation, and manifold calamities. O Lord, thou hast shown thy people hard things, and made us to drink the wine of astonishment. Because of our sins thou hast brought all these evils upon us, and given our enemies power to inflict upon us indescribable misery and irreparable wrongs. And yet, O Lord God, to whom can we fly for succor but unto thee, who hast stricken and afflicted us? O Lord, righteousness belongeth unto thee. Unto thee, O Lord God, belongeth also mercies and forgivenesses, though we have rebelled against thee. Thou keepest covenant with them that love thee, and changest not. If thy children forsake thy laws and walk not in thy judgments, then thou dost visit their transgression with the rod, and their iniquity with stripes. Nevertheless, thy loving kindness thou wilt not utterly take from them, nor suffer thy faithfulness to fail. Be it unto us now, O Lord, according to these words in which thou hast caused us to hope. Be favorable unto thy land. Forgive the iniquity of thy people, and cover all our sins. Turn us, O God of our salvation, and cause thine anger toward us to cease. Revive us again, that thy people may rejoice in thee. Show us thy mercy, and grant us thy salvation. Wilt not thou, O God, who hast cast us off, and who hast not gone out with our armies as heretofore, speak peace unto thy people, and give us help from trouble? for vain is the help of man.

We confess that we, our rulers, and our fathers have sinned against thee. We have done wickedly, and have rebelled, even by departing from thy precepts and from thy judgments. Neither have we obeyed the voice of the Lord our God, to walk in his laws which he set before us by his servants. We confess and bewail before thee, O God, that pride, prodigality, worldliness, and covetousness which is idolatry in thy sight; that profanity of thy holy name and Sabbaths; that drunkenness, gambling, and licentiousness; that irreligion, infidelity, and utter neglect of thy Word, of Christ, and of the great salvation; and that spirit of boasting and self-confident glorying, which, to so alarming an extent, prevail among us. We have slighted thy mercies, and abused thy grace and goodness to hardened impenitence, so that because sentence against sin was not exacted speedily, the hearts of many have been fully set in them to do evil. We have been forgetful of thy bounty, and regardless of thine honor. We have lived unto ourselves as if we were our own, and have not loved nor served Thee, who didst make us for thine honor and glory, who hast preserved and kept us alive, and hast bought us with the precious blood of Christ. We have sinned, O Lord, and have offended against thee. We are accused by our own consciences, and our lives testify against us. We are therefore covered with shame, and acknowledge that we are verily guilty in thy sight. Chastened as we now are by the strokes of thy providence [*here enumerate the special grounds of humiliation*], we confess that we have provoked thine anger, and although thou wert to afflict us with still severer judgments, we can only say that our crimes have deserved them all, and that Thou art a most righteous and merciful judge, who punishest not thy people without cause.

But, O Lord, thou art still doubtless our Father, and our Redeemer, who delightest in mercy. Chasten us not in fury, but in the midst of judgment remember mercy. As thou didst open a door of hope and deliverance to thy people Israel, and to our fathers when they turned unto thee, and didst avert thy chastening hand and the calamities in which they were involved, and didst never reject their prayer, nor utterly forsake or give them over to the power of their enemies, so do Thou now. Turn our hearts unto thee, O God, in unfeigned faith and sincere repentance, and turn Thyself unto us and bless us, that the whole world may acknowledge that thou art God our Saviour. Thou hast made with us an everlasting covenant, written in the blood and sealed by the death of Jesus Christ our Saviour, and now, renouncing all self-dependence and all other grounds of confidence, we fly to this blessed hope set before us. Look, therefore, O Lord, upon the face of thy Christ, and not upon us, and for the sake of His infinite merits and intercession, let thine anger be appeased, and thy face shine upon us. For His sake forgive our national, our family, our individual, and all other our sins and iniquities. Blot out our transgressions as a thick cloud, and say to us, I have forgiven you. And for thy name's sake, O God, pour out thy Holy Spirit upon us as a Spirit of repentance and reformation, and create within us new hearts, and renew a right spirit within us.

And now, O Lord, that thou hast brought thy people forth from among our enemies with a high hand, and hast ordained for them a government, and hast preserved and prospered them, and blessed their counsels and their arms, and hast gotten thee renown, now, therefore, O our God, hear the prayer of thy servants and their supplications, for the Lord's sake. Open thine eyes and behold our desolations, for we do not present our supplications before thee for our righteousness, but for thy great mercies. How long, Lord, shall our enemies ravage our inheritance and defile thy sanctuaries? Wilt thou be angry for ever? Shall thy jealousy burn like fire? O remember not against us former iniquities, but let thy tender mercies speedily prevent us, for we are brought very low. Help us, O God of our salvation, for the glory of thy Name, and deliver us, and purge away our sins. Wherefore should our enemies say, Where is their God? Let Him be known among these boastful Philistines by the revenging of the blood of thy servants which is shed. And render unto our enemies sevenfold into their bosom their reproach wherewith they have reproached thee, O Lord. So we, thy people, and sheep of thy pasture, will give thanks to Thee for ever. We will show forth thy praise to all generations.

Heavenly Father, for thy dear Son's sake, hear these our prayers. O Lord hear. O Lord forgive, hearken, and do. Defer not for thine own sake, O our God, and for the sake of thy dear Son, our Lord and Saviour Jesus Christ, in whose most blessed name and perfect form of words we further call upon thee, saying:

Our Father, who art in heaven, etc.

The grace of our Lord Jesus Christ, etc.

No. VI.

For a Revival.

O LORD, our God and Heavenly Father, thou hast taught us that as earthly parents, being evil, know how to give good gifts unto their children, much more wilt thou give thy Holy Spirit to them that ask it. O help us now so to ask that we shall receive the communications of this ever blessed Advocate, Comforter, and Sanctifier. May he be given unto us and abide with us. May he convince us of our sin in rejecting thee in thy law, and Christ in his glorious gospel. May he convince us of the divine claims of Christ, and of his cause to our love and service, by the workings of his mighty power within our hearts. May he convince us that we must all stand before the judgment seat of Christ, that we may receive, according to the deeds done while in our bodies, whether they have been good, or whether they have been evil. May he work in us to will and to do, in order that we may successfully work out our salvation with fear and trembling, giving all diligence to make our calling and election sure.

Come, thou transforming Spirit, and

breathe upon our poor, weak, sinful hearts, which are like dry bones in the valley, very many and very dry. Dead in trespasses and sins, may we be made alive unto God. Quicken us by thy life-giving power. Breathe into us the breath of spiritual life. Awaken, arouse, and revive our sluggish souls. Bring home to our minds the truth of thy holy word, that, being received into good and honest hearts, it may enlighten our eyes, make wise the simple, convert our souls, and rejoice our hearts. Make eternal realities so to rest upon us, and the terrors of the Lord so to alarm us, that we shall fly from the wrath to come, and lay hold on the hope set before us, looking unto Jesus as the author and finisher of faith, and receiving and resting upon him for salvation. May we be born again, and made new creatures in Christ Jesus.

O Lord, according to thy promise, pour out thy Holy Spirit upon our camps, upon our young men, and upon our servants. May he enlighten our understandings, and shed abroad thy love in our hearts. May he guide us into all truth. May he open blind eyes and unstop deaf ears, that we may all be converted and saved. Grant unto us the spirit of grace and supplication. Teach us to cry mightily unto thee, and to wrestle with thee, and not let thee go until thou open windows of heaven, and pour us out a blessing, so that we shall not have room to receive it.

Make this camp a Bethel. Show us thy glory as we have seen thee in the sanctuary. Wilt thou not revive us again? O Lord, revive thy work; in the midst of wrath remember mercy. Make thy word the sword of the Spirit, and sharper than any two-edged sword, and powerful in subduing the hearts of the King's enemies. May it be a discerner of the thoughts and intents of every heart, and the wisdom and power of God unto salvation. May sinners be converted unto God, and thy disciples be refreshed. May their faith be increased, their courage confirmed, and their zeal inflamed. May love to Jesus and to perishing souls fill their hearts with prayer, and their mouths with arguments. Make them wise to lead souls to Christ, and do thou seal them unto the day of redemption. Make our tents vocal with prayer and praise, so that the voice of salvation and rejoicing may be heard in the tabernacles of the righteous. May there be joy among the angels of God over many sinners that shall here repent, and in the last great day, when God maketh up his jewels, may it be said of this and that man that he was born unto God here. And, if permitted to return to our homes, may we live spiritually, and our souls prosper and be in health, so that we may be ever found useful members of thy Church, blessings to the community, and sources of religious as well as temporal benefit to our families.

Oh that thou wouldst rend the heavens and come down, that the mountains might flow down at thy presence. Put on thy strength, O arm of the Lord. Subdue the people under thee. Make them willing in this day of thy power. Confound the works of darkness, and destroy that god of this world who has blinded the eyes of sinners, lest they should hear, and be converted, and be saved. O Lord, hear. O Lord, forgive. O Lord, hearken and do. Defer not for thine own sake, O God, and for the sake of thy Son, our Lord and Saviour Jesus Christ, in whose most blessed name and perfect form of words we further call upon thee, saying—

Our Father, who art in heaven, etc.

The grace of our Lord Jesus Christ, etc.

No. VII.

Prayer for our Rulers.

ALMIGHTY and everlasting God, thou art the governor among the nations, and the ruler of heaven and earth, the fountain of wisdom, and the source and origin of all order and law, who ordaineth government for the praise, security, and comfort of those that do well, and as a terror to evil doers. Thou hast made it our duty to pray for all who are in authority over us. We desire, therefore, to bring before thee the powers that are established among us. We ask for them that wisdom that cometh down from above from the Father of light, which is profitable to direct, to instruct, to correct, and thoroughly to furnish for every good word and work. Impart unto them the spirit of wisdom, and power, and of a sound mind. O give unto them the spirit of understanding, of counsel, and right, a spirit of knowledge, and of the fear of the Lord, to make them of quick understanding. O remove not the spirit of the trusty, nor take away the understanding of the aged, nor ever let the things that belong to the nation's peace and prosperity be hidden from the eyes of those that are entrusted with the nation's counsels. Make it to appear that thou standest in the congregation of the mighty, judgest among the gods, and that when the princes of thy people and their wise men are gathered together, thou art among them. May a sense of thy presence and majesty make them suitably afraid, that all things may be done as in thy sight, to thine honor and to the glory of our land, that thou mayest be greatly exalted.

Preserve a sound mind in a sound body to our President and each member of his Cabinet, and of our national Congress, and of our state Legislatures, that they may devise wisely and execute firmly such measures as will promote the peace and prosperity of our beloved country.

We bless thee, O God, for our generals, and we would entreat thee to be round and about them, to defend and deliver them, to inspire them with skill, confidence, and courage, that, relying upon thee and guided by thy Spirit, they may be wise-hearted to discover and defeat the artifices of our enemies, to preserve the lives and secure the hearts of our soldiers, that under their guidance our armies may be made mighty through

God, to the overthrow of our enemies and the establishment of our peace, independence, and prosperity, that we may be a people saved by the Lord as the shield of our help and the sword of our excellency; and that our enemies may be sensible that God is with us, and in the midst of us, and fighteth for us.

Counsel our counsellors, and give our Senators wisdom. Make all that rule over us just, ruling in the fear of God. Let those that judge remember that they judge not for man, but for the Lord who is with them in judgment, that the fear of the Lord may be upon them. Make them able men, and men of truth, fearing God and hating covetousness, that judgment may run down like a river, and righteousness as a mighty stream.

Hear, O God, these our earnest supplications. Bless our blessings, that all nations may call us blessed, a delightsome land, and that we may be made high among the nations in praise, and in name, and in honor, by being made a holy people unto the Lord our God.

Almighty God! who hast graciously promised to hear the supplications of all who ask in thy Son's name, we beseech thee to accept the service and the prayers now offered unto thee. May those things which we have faithfully asked, according to thy will, be effectually obtained for the relief of our necessities and to the advancement of thy glory, through Jesus Christ our Lord. Amen.

Unto God's gracious mercy and protection we now commit us. The Lord bless us and keep us. The Lord make his face to shine upon us and be gracious unto us. The Lord lift up his countenance upon us, and give us peace, both now and evermore. Amen.

Our Father, who art in Heaven, etc.

The grace of our Lord Jesus Christ, etc.

No. VIII.

For our Confederacy.

O GOD, thou hast so ordained human government as to make it necessary and wise that there shall be rulers and subjects, masters and servants, rich and poor, and that these inequalities of condition and diversities of rank should be permanent and inevitable. From the beginning hitherto thou hast also, O righteous God, associated the institution of slavery as an organic form of involuntary labor with thy Church and people, thereby securing for slaves religious teaching and provision for their temporal wants, and to the world the benefit of service not otherwise attainable. Thou hast also in thy written word given us instruction as to thy will, and our duty in the relation of master and slaves, embodying this authoritative teaching and divine protection in thy holy and immutable LAW, and in the teachings of our Lord Jesus Christ and his Apostles.

By thy holy, wise, and powerful providence, O Lord, thou hast introduced slavery into these Southern states, which thou hast allotted to our fathers, and to us as a habitation for ever. Thou hast brought this people among us, and hast multiplied and blessed them, and, by their labor, their social progress, their spiritual attainments, and their conversion to God, thou hast ordained out of their mouth praise to thy great name, that the tongue of thine enemies might be stilled, and thy wonder-working providence adored. And now, O Lord, it is time for thee to work, for men have made void thy law, and teach, for thy will, the commandments of men, and philosophy, falsely so called. They consent not to wholesome words, even the words of our Lord Jesus Christ, nor to the doctrine which is according to godliness, but are proud and destitute of the truth, doting about questions whereof have come envy, strife, railing accusations against us thy people, and blasphemous speeches against thy holy Word and thy righteous name.

For the truth of thy word, O Lord, which is for ever established in the heavens; for the justice and wisdom of thine eternal providence, and thine righteousness and consistency of thy dealings with thine ancient people, Patriarchs, Prophets, and Apostles, we are persecuted, defamed, and overwhelmed with the miseries brought upon us by malicious and merciless enemies, who neither regard God nor man. But thou, O Lord, beholdest from heaven the rage and madness of this people, who have set themselves against thee, and against us who reverence thy word as the word of God, and as being all-profitable for doctrine and for instruction in righteousness. And as thou hast commanded that from such men we should withdraw ourselves, we now invoke thine omnipotent arm for our protection. O thou that art glorious in holiness, fearful in praises, a God doing wonders, in thy mercy lead forth thy people, our wives and our little ones, our men servants and our maid servants, and guide us in thy strength to thy holy habitation. Bring us in and plant us in the mountain of thine inheritance; in the place, O Lord, which thou hast made for us to dwell in, and may we know by joyful experience the blessedness of that people whose God is the Lord, and whose law is thy sure and immutable Word, free from the despotic interpretations and enforcements of men.

Establish us, therefore, O God, as a Confederacy of states, and build us up on that rock of eternal truth against which the gates of hell shall not prevail. Unite us a people in the indissoluble bonds of liberty, equality, and fraternity. Harmonize the sovereignty of our states with confederated constitutional authority. May the spirit of Washington animate them all, and lead them ever to seek not merely their own interests, but also the common good of all, and to beware of sectional jealousies and party dissensions.

Look down upon us especially as a slaveholding Confederacy. As thou hast bestowed upon us the blessing given in perpetuity to the posterity of Shem and Japhet,* do thou, in blessing, bless us, and make slavery a blessing to ourselves, to our slaves, and to the world at large. Let the blessing of Abraham, the father of the faithful and the friend of God, rest upon us and upon our servants. Pour out, as thou hast graciously promised to do, in these latter days,† the Holy Spirit upon our sons and our daughters, and upon our servants and our handmaidens, that they may call upon the Lord.

Preserve our slaves from the fanatical machinations of our enemies, who would delude and destroy them, and under the promise of liberty reduce them to poverty, barbarism, and exile from the Christian homes and happiness of their fathers. Imbue their minds with confidence in their masters, and with a spirit of cheerful and loving obedience. May they remain loyal and true, notwithstanding all the temptations with which they are assailed. Secure

---

* See Gen. ix, 25–27.
† See Acts ii, 16–18, and Joel ii, 28, 29.

to them their present religious advantages, and dispose our hearts to be more faithful to their souls, and to render unto them things just and equal.

May the issue of this war signally prove that this battle is the Lord's, and that thou hast made thy Word victorious. May atheistic blasphemy and blind fanaticism be openly rebuked, and the truth, purity, and power of thy Word, and the wisdom, equity, and mercy of thy providential dealings toward this people be gloriously established in the sight of our enemies, and before all nations throughout all generations; and may glory rest on our land until it shall be made a praise in the whole earth. Hear, O Lord, in heaven, thy dwelling place, these our humble petitions, with which we would plead and wrestle with thee. Answer them in mercy, for Christ's sake, and abundantly bless us. Grant us the desires of our hearts in accordance with thy Word; and then will we ever bless and magnify thy great and glorious name, Father, Son, and Holy Ghost. Amen and Amen.

No. IX.

The Soldiers' Prayer for their Families and Friends.*

WHILE we thus plead with thee, O Lord, for ourselves, we desire affectionately and earnestly to commend to thy divine protection and abundant mercy our absent friends and relatives. Separated from them by the command of thy providence, and the call of duty to our endangered country, be thou, O God, our Heavenly Father, their guardian and their comforter. Be thou instead of son, father, husband, brother, friend, and lover. Preserve their bodies in health and their minds in peace. Deliver them from all anxious fears for our safety and the success of our righteous cause. Inspire them with such confidence in Thee that they may calmly commit to thy most powerful, wise, and just providence all their cares and burdens. Be thou the strength of their heart and the anchor to their souls, and keep them in peace, and quietness, and assurance. Defend them from all danger. Help them in every time of need. Comfort them in all times of sickness, sorrow, and sadness. Per-

---

*To be used as a part of any prayer.

fect thy strength in their weakness, and may thy grace be sufficient for them. Guide them in every difficulty, and hear them when they ask for wisdom to direct; instruct and thoroughly furnish them for every duty devolving upon them. May their children and servants be disposed by thee to cheerful obedience and happy contentment. Provide for all their wants, and supply them out of thine infinite fulness. Secure to them kind neighbors and charitable, Christian friends. May every interest now intrusted to them prosper, and the fields yield their full increase. Let no evil come nigh their dwelling, and may ministering spirits minister unto them as heirs of salvation. Hear thou our mutual prayers, and, though sundered far, may we enjoy a sweet and sensibly felt communion around the common mercy seat. May our separation be soon terminated, and may we ere long meet and mingle as a happy band, in all the festivities of the home circle, and in all the privileges of social life, and in all the hallowed scenes of Christian worship, heavenly communion, and divine charity, each living under our own fig tree and in the enjoyment of a goodly heritage, none daring to make us afraid. Hear these our prayers, most merciful God and Father. Hasten it in our time, O Lord, that according to the days in which we have seen evil we may rejoice and be glad before thee, and may praise and bless thy glorious name, Father, Son, and Holy Ghost, all the days of our life.

Our Father, who art in heaven, etc.

The grace of our Lord Jesus Christ, etc.

No. X.

Service for a Funeral Occasion in Camp.

1. The leader will, if convenient, sing a suitable hymn.

2. He will then read a portion of Scripture.

3. The following or any suitable prayer may then be offered:

ALMIGHTY, everlasting, and ever blessed God, who art the Father of the Spirits of all flesh, thou hast taught us in thy Holy Word that affliction springeth not forth from the dust, nor cometh by chance, but that with God, the Lord, belong the issues of life and death. Thou takest away their breath; men die and return unto their dust.

Thou hast appointed to man his time upon earth, a time to be born and a time to die, so that his days are determined like the days of a hireling; and his bounds, that he cannot pass. We rejoice, O Lord, that we are thus in thine hands, who art too wise to err and too good to be unkind; that in thee we live, and move, and have our being; and that thou hast the keys of death and the grave. Blessed be the name of the Lord.

Help us, O God, while we now surround the body (*or bodies*) of our departed comrade, to acknowledge, praise, and glorify thee, to see thy providence, and hear thy voice in this solemn event; to lay it deeply to heart, to consider our own last end, and to prepare to meet our God. O may we deeply realize the solemn truth that it is appointed unto each of us once to die, and that after death cometh the judgment, when we must each one of us receive according to the deeds done in our bodies, whether they have been good or bad. O most merciful Father, who hast taken our comrade and left us, may thy goodness lead us to repentance. May a thankful remembrance of thy mercy induce us to present our bodies, souls, and spirits unto thee as a living sacrifice, and as our most reasonable service. O our Father, who hast provided for us a glorious Saviour and a gracious Comforter, and hast promised to give the Holy Spirit to them that ask, may He now work in us to will and to do of thy good pleasure, and may He lead us in the way everlasting. Make us wise unto salvation, so that in this the day of our merciful visitation we may hear the things that belong to our peace, ere they are for ever hidden from our eyes. . We know not, O God, *how*, *when*, or *where* we shall die; but we know that in the very midst of life, and strength, and manly vigor we are in death, and we cannot tell what an hour may bring forth. Grant, therefore, O holy and blessed Saviour—who for us, sinners, didst become man, and having endured the bitter pains of death, didst abolish its curse and open the kingdom of God to all believers—that, being justified by faith in thee, we may have peace with God and rejoice in hope of the glory of God.

Disarm death of its sting and the grave of its victory, and inspire us with such a sweet sense of pardoned sin, and with a hope so full of immortality, that we shall fear no evil, knowing that if any man believe in Christ, though he were dead, yet shall he live; and that if the earthly house of this tabernacle were dissolved, we have a building of God, a house not made with hands, eternal in the heavens. Save us from procrastination and presumption. May we not trust to a dying hour, nor think that patriotism is piety, or a good cause a good hope for salvation. Help us, therefore, now to fly from all refuges of lies, and lay hold on the hope set before us in the gospel. Be thou, O Christ, the anchor of our souls, the rock of our foundation; the way, the truth, and the life; our wisdom, sanctification, and redemption; our hope of glory, our all in all.

We bless thee, O Lord, that, while a long life is not always a blessing, the shortest may be sufficient to secure the great end of life—even the salvation of our souls and a life everlasting. Should we die young, or suddenly, as in a moment, may we not die unprepared; nor until, by faith, we have seen the Lord Christ, and know that our Redeemer liveth, and that, although after death worms may destroy these bodies, yet in our flesh we shall see God, whom we shall see for ourselves, and our eyes behold him. Give us grace while living to prepare for dying, and when dying for dying in the Lord, that our last end may be peace. When heart and flesh shall fail us, be thou, O Lord, the strength of our heart. Amid the brief agonies of a violent death do thou, our Saviour, who didst endure the slow tortures of the cross, succor us with thy peace: that peace which the world can neither give nor take away; which passeth all understanding, and which can make even a gory bed feel soft as downy pillows are, while on thy breast we lean our head and breathe our soul out sweetly there. Though alone, and far from loving ones at home, may Thy presence be with us, and may Thy consolations delight our souls. Receive into thine hands our departing spirit. Cheer it with the prospect of victory beyond the grave, and a crown of glory that fadeth not away. May our death be precious in thy sight. May our parting soul be made perfect in holiness, and fitted for an inheritance among the spirits of the just. Borne by angels' wings to Abraham's bosom, may we find that to be absent from the body is to be present, that very day in Paradise, with thee our ever blessed Lord and Saviour.

We thank thee, O God, who art thyself a man of war, and the God of battles, and the giver of victory, for the patriotism, valor, willingness to die, and manly fortitude of our fallen heroic brethren. May their names live in the everlasting remembrance of a redeemed and grateful country, and irradiate their posterity with glory. God of our Fathers, and God of Nations, may their blood cry not in vain for vengeance on the perjured, hypocritical, and blood-thirsty heads of our tyrannical oppressors. May their blood kindle into a flame our burning patriotism; dispel fear, and arouse the spirit of a noble daring, that we may emulate their example and secure for them the graves of freedom, or perish with them in the death struggle for liberty. God of our Fathers and of our Warriors, let no enslaved race of freemen ever live on soil made holy by the graves of our martyred dead. O Father! Father of our Fathers! and of these slaughtered children of our Fathers! who didst give to them this goodly heritage, and impart to them a love for liberty stronger than the love of life, nerve our hearts to contend earnestly unto blood for our homes and hearths, for our wives and our sisters, for our sanctuaries and cemeteries, for our holy religion, and for thy glory, O God, and to swear upon thine altar, and over the ashes of our buried comrades—who have put off their mortal clothing and put on the immortal, and are now crowned with victory—that while the soil of our country is polluted by the tread of a barbarous foe we will either live with her, or die for her.

Oh God! who art not unrighteous in taking vengeance, we, thy oppressed and outraged people, do now cry unto thee. Behold our tears; our wrongs; our desecrated temples, our imperiled cities, liberties, and religion; all that thou hast given us, and made dear to us as our own lives; and answer us from thy secret place of thunder. Make thyself known by the judgments which thou executest against them who make might right, and, with perjured hearts and profane lips, seek to overwhelm us in the ruins of a constitutional government which their faithless fanaticism has destroyed. Arise, O God, Judge of the earth! Cause judgment to be heard from heaven. Thou that sittest on the throne, judging right, maintain our righteous cause. Be a refuge to the oppressed. Make inquisition for blood, and remember thy slaughtered children. Arise, O Lord, let not our enemies prevail. Rebuke them. Put them in fear. Turn them back, and may they perish at thy presence. May the stars in their courses fight against them, and the angel of death pursue them. Arise, O Lord God of Hosts! Awake! put on thy strength, and lift us up from the gates of death, that we may rejoice in thy salvation, and praise thee in the midst of thy temple.

And now, almighty and everlasting God, we commit this body of our deceased comrade to the earth, in joyful hope of a glorious resurrection. And in that great and awful day, when thou, the righteous Judge, shalt come to judge the quick and the dead, grant, O most merciful Father, that we may be found of thee in peace. O Lord God of Hosts! hear our prayer; give ear, O God of Jacob. Behold, O God, our shield, and look upon the face of thine Anointed. So we, thy people and the sheep of thy pasture, will give thee thanks for ever; we shall show forth thy praise through all generations. Amen.

Our Father, who art in heaven, etc.

The grace of our Lord and Saviour, etc.

No. XI.

Prayer against our Enemies and for Peace.

O GOD, unto whom all hearts are open, and all desires known, we come unto thee, and fall down before thee, and worship thee, whose power is infinite, whose wisdom is unsearchable, and whose providence extendeth over all things and all events. Thou art the high and mighty ruler of the universe, who doest whatsoever thou pleasest among the armies of heaven and the inhabitants of earth, none daring, with impunity, to resist thy will, or to say unto thee What doest Thou?

Great and terrible God! thy judgments are now devastating this once fair, fertile, and prosperous Union of free, sovereign, and independent states. Thou hast brought upon us this war which is the sword of thy vengeance, and given it a commission to execute the fierceness of thy wrath upon a guilty land, and to divide us into separate and independent countries for ever.

We plead before thee, O God, the righteousness of our cause. Our confederates have broken the covenant made with them by our Fathers and sealed in the chancery of heaven. They have dealt treacherously with us, their brethren, in these Southern states, and perfidiously deprived us of impartial justice, equal rights, guaranteed protection and honorable security for our slaves whom thou hast brought among us, and given us charge over them, for good to them and to the world, and for glory to thy holy, wise, and powerful providence. They have perverted thy truth and prostituted thy holy religion, and usurped thy supreme prerogative as Lord of conscience; and, while we invoked a peaceful separation, they have taken the sword, and blown the trumpet of war, and have come up against us to subdue us, and to rule impiously over us, making void thy law and enforcing for thy doctrines the commandments of men.

We acknowledge, O thou righteous Judge eternal, that while our enemies are the hand the sword is thine. They have no power at all against us but that which thou hast given them, and thou art able to stay their vengeance, and to punish them for their horrid cruelties, their diabolic malice, and their barbarous vandalism. The nations have heard of their shame; and the cry of our miseries, and of unparalleled atrocities perpetrated among us, has filled the whole civilized world, and is continually ascending unto thee, O righteous Father, to whom belongeth vengeance. Wherefore hast thou, O Lord, done this against our land? What meaneth the heat of this great anger? How long, O Lord, holy, just, and true, dost thou not avenge us speedily against these our enemies? We acknowledge our sins, and the sins of our fathers, and the righteousness of thy chastening judgments. We are sinners before thee, O God, and we dwell among a sinful people. But, Lord, be not very wroth. Let not thine anger endure for ever. In wrath remember mercy, and let it repent thee concerning thy servants. Turn away thine anger, and be reconciled unto us and restore us.

Hear, most merciful Father, the prayer of multitudes who sigh and cry for the abominations of our land, and for thine own Name's sake turn away ungodliness from our people and pour out upon them a spirit of repentance, reformation, and godliness. Thou hast caused us to hope in thy Word. Thou hast given us a banner to be displayed because of the truth. Arise, O God, and plead our cause against a faithless and fanatical people. The battle is thine, O Lord God of truth and justice. Vindicate thy Word, will, and providence. Let not their counsel stand, neither let it come to pass. Though they associate themselves, let them be broken in pieces, and though they take counsel together, speak thou the word, O Lord, and it shall come to nought. For thy power standeth not in multitude, nor thy might in strong men; for thou art a God of the afflicted, a helper of the oppressed, an upholder of the weak, a protector of the forlorn, and a Saviour of them that are without hope.

How long, O Lord, shall we hear the sound of the trumpet and the clang of arms? Thou didst bring this war upon us, and Thou canst deliver us from it. May it please thee in thy merciful goodness, O Lord, who makest wars to cease to the ends of the earth, to ordain peace for us. Grant unto us speedily, we beseech thee, peace; a righteous, honorable, and propitious peace. Give unto us, thou Sovereign disposer of all events, this peace in our time, before we are cut off from the land of the living and go hence to be no more.

O Lord God, to whom belongeth righteousness, and mercies, and forgivenesses, though we have rebelled against thee—who hast brought thy people forth with thy right hand, and hast gotten thee renown as at this day—let thine anger and thy fury be turned away from us, and cause thy face to shine upon our land which is desolate, for the Lord's sake. Send now peace and prosperity. Save us from our enemies, and from the hands of all that hate us, that we being delivered out of the hand of our enemies might serve thee without fear. O our God, incline thine ear and hear, and open thine eyes and behold our desolations. For we do not present our supplications before thee for our righteousnesses, but for thy great mercies. O Lord hear, O Lord forgive, O Lord hearken and do; defer not for thine own sake, O my God. Thy people are called by thy name.

*[Look down from heaven upon thy desolate sanctuaries; upon thy people dispersed and persecuted; and upon the lambs of thy flock scattered upon the mountains, and far from thy pastures and their Shepherd's care.

---

* The part within brackets may be omitted or used at pleasure.

We pray, O Lord, for the peace and prosperity of Zion, that peace may again dwell within her gates, and prosperity within her palaces. Bring forth her exiled bands, restore her waste places, heal her breaches, rebuild her broken walls, and add to her multitudes of such as shall be saved. Pour out thy spirit upon her sons and her daughters, upon her old men and mothers, and upon her servants. And may our children be seen flocking as doves to their windows, numerous as the drops of dew in the womb of the morning. May those that have been panting in desert places like the hart for the water brooks, again appear before thee, the living God, and again flourish in the courts of the Lord, and bring forth fruit unto old age. And may thy people again be glad in going up to the house of God in company with multitudes who attend upon thy solemn feasts.

Look upon our families, O thou who placest the solitary in families and lovest all the dwellings of thine Israel, and again reunite them around their own hearths, under their own vine and fig tree, none daring to make them afraid; that the incense of prayer may ascend up to thee continually from every family altar and from the altar of many hearts.

Look down upon our schools, colleges, and seminaries of theological learning which are now languishing or disbanded, and speedily reopen their closed gates of knowledge; and fill them with numerous aspirants after public usefulness in thy vineyard and in their country's service, who shall become eminent for wisdom, statesmanship, and piety, and exalt the fame of our country and the glory of thy Church.

Look upon our cities now silent, burnt with fire, and ravaged with the sword, and may they again become populous, and commerce be revived, and prosperity abound, and may all our streets say hallelujah and praise Thee, saying: Blessed be God, who hath redeemed them for ever.

Look upon our fields laid waste, our gardens converted into deserts, and our barns empty; and may the earth again bring forth abundantly, and the wilderness blossom as the rose, and our barns be filled with plenty of the finest of the wheat. Look, O God of pitiful compassion and tender sympathy, upon bereaved families and broken hearts, and be thou the husband of the widow and the father of the fatherless. Take up, O Lord, those who are forsaken and forlorn, and give beauty for ashes, the oil of joy for mourning, the garment of praise for the spirit of heaviness.]

Merciful God, who didst proclaim peace on earth, who art thyself the God of peace, and of hope, and consolation, O do thou now impart peace to thy distressed people. Almighty Saviour, who art the Prince of peace, who camest to bring peace on earth and good will to men, and to reunite in bonds of peace God with man, and man with man, do thou command these raging waves of war to be at peace, and there shall be a great calm. O holy and ever blessed Spirit, the Comforter, whose fruits within the soul are peace, gentleness, brotherly kindness, and tender compassion, send peace into the hearts of our enemies, and so work in them to will and to do that they shall seek the things that make for peace, and be glad to be at peace with us. O God, who art over all and blessed for ever, Father, Son, and Holy Ghost, satisfy us early with thy mercy, that we may rejoice and be glad all our days. Make us glad according to the days wherein thou hast afflicted us, and the days wherein we have seen evil. Fill our mouth with laughter and our tongue with singing, that it may be said among the nations, the Lord hath done great things for us. Help, Lord, and save us for thy mercies' sake. O Lord God of Hosts, hear our prayer. Give ear, O God of Jacob. Behold, O God, our shield, and look upon the face of thine Anointed. According unto the multitude of thy mercies—according to the riches of thy grace, for thine own sake, O Lord, and for thy Christ's sake, be merciful unto us sinners, to the glory of thy rich and sovereign mercy in Christ Jesus. Amen.

Our Father, who art in heaven, etc.

The grace of our Lord Jesus Christ, etc.

No. XII.

Prayer for a Thanksgiving for Peace.

THOU, O Lord, art Governor among the nations. Thou judgest the world in righteousness, and ministerest judgment to the people in uprightness. Surely, O God, thou hast beheld the affliction of thy people, and heard their cry, and known their sorrow. For the misery of the poor, for the sighing of the needy, for the prayer of the widow and the fatherless; for the cry of innocent blood, shed by wicked and ruthless hands in every part of our blood-stained soil, thou hast arisen, O Lord; and He that is higher than the highest has avenged us on these, our adversaries, and recompensed their own way upon their heads. Because they have warred against thy people by taking vengeance, and have greatly offended because they have avenged themselves upon us with despiteful hearts, and have shed the blood of thy children by force in the time of our calamity, Thou hast prepared them unto blood, and made blood pursue them, that they may know that thou art the Lord. When thy hand was lifted up, O Lord, they would not see; but they have seen and are made ashamed for their envy at thy people; yea, the fire of thine anger has devoured them. Righteous art thou, O Lord, when thou judgest! Hallelujah! for the Lord God omnipotent reigneth, and doth according to the counsel of his will, to the praise of his own glory.

O God, whose name alone is Jehovah, and who art the most high over all the earth; thou art our God, and we will praise thee, our fathers' God; and we will exalt thee, the Rock of ages, with whom is everlasting strength, and the memorial of whose goodness is unto all generations. Thy right hand, O Lord, is become glorious in power. Thy right hand, O Lord, has dashed in pieces the enemy. And in the greatness of thine excellency thou hast overthrown them that rose up against us. This is the Lord's doing, and it is marvellous in our eyes. O God, who art the God of peace, thou hast ordained peace for us. Lord, thou hast been favorable unto thy land. Thou hast forgiven the iniquity of thy people; thou hast covered all their sins. Thou in thy mercy hast led forth the people whom thou hast redeemed; thou hast guided them in thy strength unto thy holy habitation; thou hast increased the nation, O Lord; thou hast increased the nation; thou art glorified. Thou has brought them in, and planted them in the mountain of thine inheritance, in the place, O Lord, which thou hast made for thee to dwell in, the sanctuary, O Lord, which thy hands have established. May we trust in the Lord for ever, for in the Lord Jehovah is everlasting strength. For he bringeth down them that dwell on high; the lofty nation he layeth it low even to the ground, he bringeth it even to the dust. In the way of thy judgments, O Lord, have we waited for thee; the desire of our soul is to thy name, and to the remembrance of thee. Who is like unto thee, O Lord, among the gods? Who is like unto Thee, glorious in holiness, fearful in praises, doing wonders?

Now, O Lord, that thou hast turned again our captivity, we are like those that dream. The night season of terrible calamity and frightful apprehensions has passed, and we awake to see the sunshine of peace, prosperity, and plenty shine all around us. Thy voice of mercy speaketh peace unto thy people. Thou makest assured peace in our borders and feedest us with the finest of the wheat. Thou hast filled our mouths with laughter and our tongues with singing. Thou hast wiped away all tears from off all faces.

We would remember, O Lord, the days that are past, the years in which we have seen evil; when thou didst feed thy people on the bread of adversity, and give them wormwood and gall to drink; and didst fill our land with the wail of sorrow. We sat down, yea, we wept, when we remembered Zion. We would not forget all Thy mercies toward us, and thy gracious benefits then so freely conferred upon us in sustaining, succoring, and comforting us. We would recount them over and over, and call upon our souls and all within us to be stirred up worthily to magnify and bless thy name. We give thanks unto the Lord, who has remembered us in our low estate, and has redeemed us from our enemies, for thy mercy endureth for ever. We praise thee with our whole heart for thy loving kindness and for thy truth. In the day when we cried unto thee thou answeredst us and strengthenedst us with strength in our soul. Though we walked in the midst of trouble, thou didst revive us. Thou didst stretch forth thine hand against the wrath of our enemies, and thy right hand saved us. Praise waiteth for thee, O God, in Zion. In the midst of thy temple we will think of all thy loving kindness. From the uttermost parts of our land thou shalt hear songs of rejoicing. With our wives and our little ones, and with our heroic dead, who are still ours to love and honor them in the blessed and holy communion of all saints in heaven, we unite this day in descriptions of glory. We thank thee for these our martyred sons who are now to become our fathers, and live in everlasting remembrance in the annals of our war and in the hearts of a generous and grateful country. May their bereaved families find in thee a covenant-keeping God, and in our people nursing fathers and nursing mothers.

And now, O God, who by thy Word and Spirit hast created this United Confederacy, and hast now established its independence, and sent it forth in the career of political existence, baptized by the blood of thousands of the best and bravest of her sons, and cemented into one body by the common loss of prosperity and property, and the common endurance of a great fight of affliction, wilt thou not become our guardian, guide, and governor. Set up in our midst thy throne of justice and righteousness. Come and reign over us. Rule in our minds and hearts by thy Word, will, and providence. Make thy glory our chief end, and thy Word our infallible standard of right and wrong, of truth, and duty. Most merciful God, who hast done so great things for us, let us not be satisfied with triumphant success of arms, political and military glory, or with agricultural, commercial, and social prosperity. Save us, save us, O God, from vainglorious pride and self-reliance, and from all worldliness and ungodliness. Leave, O leave us not to ourselves, to carnal reason, selfish policy, or mere material aggrandizement. Go up with us, and keep near to us, and dwell among us, and be not as a wayfaring man or as a stranger in the land. Pour out upon us thy Spirit. Revive among us thy work. Diffuse throughout our land pure and undefiled religion. Exalt our nation by righteousness, and make it Emmanuel's land, and may we be that happy people whose God is the Lord.

Preserve us, O God, from international jealousy and strife; from party spirit, sectional rivalry, and political ambition. O God, who art the ruler of heaven and earth, be thou our pilot through the storm-tossed deep, covered as it is with the wrecks of so many foundered nations. Guide us securely through the rocks and quicksands on which they perished; and may heavenly wisdom direct our people in the safe course which will lead to permanent prosperity and peace.

Rule Thou in the hearts of our rulers; counsel our counsellors; and give to our Senators, our Congressional and State Legislatures, and to all Judges, Governors, and Magistrates, and to all who have influence or authority over us, the spirit of power and of a sound mind, the spirit of counsel and of might, and of the fear of the Lord. Make them able men, and men of truth, fearing God and hating covetousness, that judgment may run down like a river and righteousness like a mighty stream. Give grace to all citizens to live quiet and peaceable lives in all godliness and honesty, dwelling in peace and unity, that the Lord may command a blessing upon us, and life for evermore.

Let our schools, colleges, and seminaries be replenished with every good and perfect gift from the Father of lights. Cast the salt of thy grace into these fountains, that the streams thereof may make glad the city of our God, the holy place of the tabernacles of the Most High. Bless all classes and conditions of men among us—the high and the low, the rich and the poor, the learned and unlearned, the free and the bond, the servant and the master.

We pray, O Lord our God, for the peace and prosperity of Zion. May she arise out of all these troubles and shine, the glory of the Lord having risen upon her. May the blood of her martyrs prove the seed of the Church. Having gone forth weeping, may she now come again rejoicing and bearing her sheaves with her. May a spirit of humility, penitence, and unfeigned faith be poured out upon all our disbanded soldiers. May thy goodness toward them during all their dangers and distresses lead them to a grateful consecration of their spared lives unto the Lord, so that in return for all His benefits they may take the cup of salvation and pay their vows unto him who loved them and gave Himself for them.

And now the Lord our God be with *us*, as he was with our fathers. Let him not leave us nor forsake us, that he may incline our hearts unto him to keep his commandments, and his statutes, and his judgments, that our hearts may be perfect with the Lord our God all our days. We present these our imperfect prayers and most unworthy services in the all-prevailing name of Jesus, who died for our sins and rose again for our justification, and who ever liveth to make intercession for us, to whom be honor and dominion everlasting. Amen.

Our Father, who art in Heaven, etc.

The grace of our Lord Jesus Christ, etc.

PERSONAL AND PRIVATE PRAYERS.

No. I.

For One who is a Professor of Religion.

THY vows, O God, are upon me. I have subscribed my name unto the Lord, and entered into covenant with thee. I have taken the cup of salvation into my hand, and paid my vows unto thee in the presence of the great congregation. I have given myself unto thee, O Lord, and then to thy Church, according to the will of God. I have taken thy yoke upon me, and have felt it to be easy, glorying in thy cross, and rejoicing to be counted worthy to be thy disciple and follower. I would remember with gratitude and praise the time when first I found thee, O Lord—the time of my espousals, when I said unto my soul, "Thou art my portion, O Lord, truly I am thy servant," and when thou didst say unto me, "I am thy God and Saviour, I have loved thee, and chosen thee, and united thee to myself, and have put my Name upon thee, and my Spirit within thee, and sealed thee unto the day of redemption, and I will never leave nor forsake thee." How sweet, O Lord, the memory of those transporting hours, when thou didst bring me into thy banqueting house and thy banner over me was love; when I felt no longer as a stranger, or a guest, but as a child at home, and did eat, and drink in thy presence, and partake of the feast of fat things thy mercy has prepared for them that love thee.

O most merciful God and Father, it is with shame, and confusion of face, and with an aching void in my cold, careless, worldly heart I now come before thee. The thoughts of thy loving kindness, thy tender mercy, and thy forgiving love bring tears to my eyes and sorrow to my heart when I consider how ungrateful I have been, how prone to wander forgetful of my highest love, my best friend, and my most satisfying joy. And now, O Lord, I am in circumstances of peculiar difficulty and danger to my soul. Away from home, separated from Christian friends, deprived of the accustomed means of grace, surrounded by temptations; exposed to evil example and corrupt communications, to all the devices of Satan, the lusts of the flesh, and the pride of life, I am greatly tempted to restrain prayer before God, and to forget and forsake Thee utterly.

Forsake me not, O God of my salvation. Take not thy Holy Spirit from me. Make thy grace sufficient for me, and perfect strength in my weakness. Restore my soul. Revive my love and affections toward thee. Rekindle the flame of my first, happy, heavenly love. Reanimate my faith, and hope, and peace, and joy. Inspire me with courage, confidence, and affection. Fill me with zeal for thine honor and glory, and for the salvation of souls. Create in me a clean heart, and renew a right spirit within me. Deliver me from the spirit of unmanly fear and shame in confessing thee before men, and let not the praise of men or the honor that cometh from men deprive me of Thy favor, which is life, and of that honor that cometh from thee, which is better than life. Restore unto me the joys of thy salvation, and satisfy me with thy mercy, that I may rejoice and be glad before thee. As I have received the Lord Jesus, do thou enable and dispose me to esteem it my interest, privilege, happiness, and duty to walk and to live with Him. Enable me, O Lord, to hold fast mine integrity, and to keep myself unspotted from the world. Keep me from falling, and uphold me by thy free Spirit; that by a holy, consistent, humble walk and conversation I may prove the gospel to be all divine, adorn the doctrine of God my Saviour, and glorify him who bought me with his precious blood, in my body, soul, and spirit, which are his. Strengthen me with all might in the inner man that I may contend earnestly and fight manfully the good fight of faith, and wrestle hard not only with flesh and blood, but with principalities and powers. Clothe me with the whole armor of God, that, having done all thy holy will, and lived to thine honor and glory, I may come off a conqueror, and more than a conqueror, through him that loved me, and gave Himself for me, to whom, with thee, O Father, and the Holy Ghost, be all honor, and glory, and blessing, both now and for ever. Amen.

Our Father, who art in heaven, etc.

The grace of our Lord and Saviour, etc.

No. II.

For a Backslider.

MOST holy, blessed, and gracious God, on whom is all my dependence, and from whom is all my hope and expectation, I am ashamed, and blush to appear before thee from whom I have so often and so grievously wandered, and whose long suffering and patience I have so long abused by my wayward, worldly, and wicked course. I have forsaken thine ordinances, neglected thy Word, and profaned thy Sabbaths. I have restrained prayer, cast off fear, and, having loved this present evil world, have lived unto myself, and not unto Him who died for me, and rose again for my justification, and who ever liveth to make intercession for me. I know not how to lift up my eyes unto heaven, for I have provoked Thee to anger and jealousy by trifling with thy love, grieving thy Holy Spirit, trampling under foot the blood of the everlasting covenant, and by thus crucifying afresh the blessed Saviour and putting him to an open shame. God be merciful to me a sinner. I am without excuse, and speechless before thee. I acknowledge my transgressions which I have, from time to time, committed against thee, against light and love; and against my own knowledge and conscious guilt; and in manifesting such base ingratitude, unbelief, and ungodliness.

I have often resolved and promised that I would return from the error of my ways unto Thee the good and gracious Shepherd of my soul; but I have again broken my faith and relapsed into my former carelessness and open sin; and have thus trifled with thy long enduring and compassionate forbearance, and forfeited all claim to thy promised mercy. Wert thou, therefore, O holy and righteous Saviour, to enter into judgment with me, and to require an account of my stewardship, I could not stand before thee. But may I not, O most merciful Saviour, fly from the bar of thy justice to the throne of thy grace, beseeching thee to show pity and forgiveness to me, because thou delightest in mercy and art able to save to the uttermost all that come unto God by thee? Thou hast assured me by thy word and by my own past experience that, as a father pities and forgives his offending child, so dost thou yearn over thy prodigal children, and have compassion on them, and draw them back to thee by the cords of love. I know, O Lord, that thy tender mercies are over all thine other works, and that thine arm of mercy and heart of love are ever open to receive returning wanderers to thy fold. O God of all power, O God of mercy and compassion, reclaim and restore my soul. Say not that I am joined to my idols, let him alone. Leave me not to my own heart's lusts nor to the wiles of the Devil. Give me not up to obduracy and impenitence. Forsake me not, despise me not, O God of salvation. Take not thy Holy Spirit from me. Come to my help, O thou who art the hope of Israel and the Saviour thereof in time of trouble. Thou didst come to call sinners to repentance; to seek and save the lost; to die for the ungodly; to impart thy grace and gifts even to the rebellious; to save the chief of sinners; and in no wise to cast out any that come unto Thee. Quicken my soul that I may run after thee. Wilt thou not revive me again, and renew me unto repentance and godly sorrow, and heal all my backslidings, and love me freely? Wash me thoroughly from my iniquities, and restore unto me the joy of thy salvation; my early faith; my first love; my ardent hope; my exultant confidence; my jubilant anticipations; my soul-refreshing intercourse and communion with Thee, in all the means of thy grace; my ardent zeal and cheerful delight in the keeping of thy commandments, and in doing and suffering all thy righteous will.

Cleanse me from all filthiness of the flesh and spirit. Set me free from the bondage of corruption and the sins that do so easily beset me. O help me against the power of prevailing iniquity. If thou wilt, thou canst make me willing, working in me both to will and to do of thy good pleasure. Thou who didst justify the Publican, and hear the prayer of the thief on the cross, listen to this my penitential confession. Manasseh sinned, but, having repented, was forgiven. David also sinned, but when he sought forgiveness he obtained mercy. Peter denied thee and fell, but was restored by thy look of transforming power. Thou didst make Paul a pattern of mercy unto all who should hereafter believe. Comfort, then, and convert my soul, Father of mercies and God of all consolation. Make this camp (*or hospital, or tent*) a Bethel where I shall meet with, and be reconciled to God. Make it a Bochim, a place of penitential tears, earnest prayer, and reanimated faith and hope. May its duties, difficulties, and dangers, its temptations and trials, drive me more helplessly to Thee who canst make them all helps and not hinderances, a daily discipline, and a means and opportunity of doing good. Let Thy grace be sufficient for me. Perfect strength in my weakness. Uphold me by thy free Spirit, and keep me by thy power through faith unto salvation.

Hear my prayer, O Lord. As a backsliding child I have heard thy voice and come unto thee. Restore, therefore, and strengthen thy servant, that a sense of pardoning mercy and constraining love may enable and dispose me to proclaim thy grace to others; that sinners may be converted unto Thee, and that I may serve thee henceforward with joy and alacrity; and be daily growing in meekness for the hour of my departure, and for an inheritance among the saints made perfect, that, with the innumerable multitude of the redeemed, I may evermore ascribe all glory and praise unto Him who loved me, and washed me in his own precious blood.

Our Father, who art in heaven, etc.

The grace of our Lord and Saviour, etc.

No. III.

Prayer of a Sinner for Mercy, Repentance, and Faith.

OMNISCIENT, omnipresent, and heart-searching God, all things are naked and open unto thee with whom I have to do. Thou art acquainted with all my ways. Thou knowest my thoughts afar off, and my heart, and life, and character; my down-sitting and my uprising, my outgoing and my incoming are not hidden from thy sight. It is in Thee I live, and move, and have my being, and, as thou hast appointed the bounds of my life, and the hour of my death, so when thou sayest return, my body shall return unto the dust from which it sprang, and my soul unto thee who gave it, that I may receive according to the deeds done while in my body, whether they have been good or evil.

O God, thou righteous Judge eternal, convert my inmost soul. Impress deeply upon my thoughtless heart the reality and infinite importance of eternal things. Bring the future near. Make things invisible to mortal eyes clear and certain to my spiritual vision. Awaken and arouse me to a full conviction of the uncertainty of life, the nearness and certainty of death, and of that judgment which is after death. May my eyes be opened to see, and my ears to hear, and my heart to feel, and my conscience to condemn, that, ere it be too late, I may be converted and saved. May thy goodness lead me to repentance, and the terrors of the Lord persuade me to turn unto thee that Thou mayest have mercy upon me. What shall it profit me, O God, if I gain the whole world and lose my own soul, or what could I give in exchange for my soul if lost? O that in this, the day of my merciful visitation, I may be enabled and disposed to attend to the things that belong to my everlasting peace, before they are for ever hidden from my eyes.

I am a sinful man, O God. My own heart condemns me, and thou art greater than my heart, and knowest all things. O God, thou knowest my foolishness, and my sins are not hid from thee. I am a sinner, O God, and one of the chief of sinners. I was born in sin and prone to evil, and I went astray from the womb speaking lies. Thou, O God, hast not been in all my thoughts, to love and serve thee. I have set thee at naught, and cast off all fear of thee, and have lived without thee and without hope in the world. I have shamefully neglected those things which I ought to have done, and as shamelessly done those things which I ought not to have done. I have abused thy goodness and mercy which ought to have led me to repentance, by abounding in sin, and living unto myself, seeking my own pleasure and profit, following the desires and devices of my own evil heart, loving this present evil world, and living according to its fashion in the lusts of the flesh, the lusts of the eyes, and the pride of life. I have thus made an idol of myself, and a god of my belly, and have gloried in my shame, worshipping and serving the creature more than the Creator, who is God over all and blessed for ever. And I have thus acted against all the endearments of thy mercies and terrors of thy wrath; against all the striving of thy spirit, and admonitions of thy providence, and warnings of my own conscience.

Lord, be merciful unto me a presumptuous, ungrateful, false, faithless, desperately blind, and foolish sinner. Have mercy upon me, O God, and blot out my transgressions. Wash me thoroughly from my iniquity, and cleanse me from my sin. For I acknowledge my transgressions, and my sin is ever before me.

And yet, O God, thou hast borne with me, and hast had patience, and hast not cast me off in the midst of my sins, and suddenly destroyed me without remedy. Let my prayer therefore, O Lord, come before thee in this acceptable time, when I may be heard and saved. O God, in the multitude of thy mercy hear me, according to the greatness of thy salvation. Hear me, O Lord, for thy loving kindness is good. Hide not thy face from thy servant, for I am in trouble. Hear me speedily. Draw nigh unto my soul, and redeem and deliver it. Work in me a full conviction of my guilt and misery. Open my heart to receive, and to feel thy grace, and mercy, and forgiving love. Behold me, O Lord, at thy mercy seat pleading guilty and surrendering myself to thee, from whom I cannot escape. I have not one word to offer in my vindication or excuse. Neither can I understand nor describe the enormity and wickedness of my sins, as committed against the glory of thine infinite majesty, the unspeakable preciousness of the blood of thy dear Son, and the boundless love and graciousness of the ever blessed Spirit. O God, thy love and long-suffering patience in waiting still to be gracious to me that my soul may live, and not die eternally, is marvellous. Save therefore now, I beseech thee, O God of my salvation. Convince, convert, and regenerate my soul. I ask forgiveness, O Father, and hope for it only because of thy abundant, free, and sovereign mercies, and the infinite merits of thy most gracious, compassionate, and all-sufficient Saviour, and the illimitable, condescending tenderness of the Holy Ghost the Comforter. Now, therefore, O God, give me faith, repentance, and power to turn unto thee with my whole heart, and to yield myself, body, soul, and spirit, unto thee, a living sacrifice, that I may live the rest of my life unto Him that loved me and gave himself for me, so that to me to live may be Christ, and to die gain. Grant these petitions, O most merciful God, through the merits and mediation of thy only Son, and my only Saviour and Redeemer Jesus Christ. Amen.

Our Father, who art in heaven, etc.

The grace of our Lord Jesus Christ, etc

No. IV.

For a Sick or Wounded Soldier.

MOST gracious and merciful God, thou dost not willingly afflict the children of men, neither dost thou hide thy face from them, but dost hear when they cry unto thee. With thee are the issues of life and death. Thou bringest down to the grave, and art able to restore again to health, and to heal all our diseases, and renew our strength like the eagle's. I rejoice, O Father, that I can look to thee in my present painful affliction, and feel that it does not spring from the dust, nor come upon me by chance, but that it is ordered and overruled by thy holy, wise, and gracious providence. I resign myself therefore wholly to thy guidance, and cast myself upon thy mercy. O merciful Father, make me to hear thy voice, saying unto me as to a son, My son despise not thou the chastening of the Lord, neither faint when thou art rebuked of him. O Lord, as a son, I would learn obedience, and yield to thee an affectionate and confiding submission. I would now arise, and come unto thee, my most gracious and pitiful Father, and say, Father, I have sinned against thee, and provoked thy just displeasure. But with thee there is plenteous redemption, and as it is thy property, so thou delightest to have mercy. Have compassion upon me, thy poor, prodigal son, and receive and restore me to thy favor, and my long lost home and happiness.

I know, O Lord, that thou canst do all things, and, if it is consistent with thine all-wise arrangement, thou canst look upon me, and forthwith I shall live, and recover strength before I go hence and be no more; and that, if not, thou canst make thy grace sufficient for me, and enable me to resign life, health, and happiness to thy disposal, and to say, Father, thy will be done. I know that all thy judgments are right, that thou doest all things well, and that in very faithfulness thou dost afflict me. But, O Lord, I am sinful and full of fears. I am unprepared to stand before thy judgment seat, and therefore I am afraid to die. I am oppressed. My soul is cast down within me, and I cannot so much as lift up mine eyes to heaven. God be merciful to me a sinner. In weakness and in misery I cast myself at thy feet. I am without excuse. Neither would I cloak nor dissemble my offences, which are all naked and open unto thee, O holy, omniscient, and righteous God! with whom I have now to do, and who art able to cast soul and body into hell for ever. O Thou, who art the hope of sinners and their Saviour in time of trouble, intercede for me, and give me repentance and remission of sins. Thou who art mighty to save to the uttermost all who come unto God by thee, and who art not willing that any should perish, but that all should come unto thee and live, do Thou undertake for me, and have mercy upon me. Say unto my soul, I am thy salvation. Convince, convert, and comfort me by thy Holy Spirit. Give me a new heart and a humble, contrite, and believing spirit. Pardon all my innumerable sins of heart and life. Cleanse me from their guilt, power, and pollution. Justify me freely for thine own Name's sake, that I may have peace with God, through thee, my Lord and Saviour Jesus Christ.

I acknowledge, O Lord, that while the stroke of thy hand is heavy upon me, and the sufferings I deserve, and have feared, have come upon me, that in wrath thou rememberest mercy. Thou hast not dealt with me according to my sins nor rewarded me according to my iniquities. Thou mightest have driven me away in my wickedness, and destroyed me suddenly, and given no opportunity for repentance, nor for calling upon thee for grace and mercy. I bless thee for this sure token of thy loving kindness and willingness to save me ere it be too late. May it be so, O Lord! Grant me that godly sorrowing for sin that shall not need to be repented of. I would love thee, O blessed Saviour, who didst so love me as to give thyself for me, and didst redeem me—not with gold and silver, but with thine own precious blood—let thy love be so shed abroad in my heart as to constrain me to love Thee. Take this poor, weak, sinful heart, and make it thine. Seal, sanctify, and save it. Cast not a trembling, helpless sinner from thy presence, neither take thy Holy Spirit from me. Glorify thyself in me as the helper of the helpless and the Saviour of the lost, that the bones which thou hast broken may rejoice, and my sinking spirits may be lifted up with hope in God, and rejoice in the fulness of the blessings of the gospel of Christ.

If it be thy blessed will, relieve my pains, remove my sickness, and restore my health, that I may live to serve and glorify Thee, with my body and spirit, which are thine. But should this sickness be unto death, impart unto me a holy, happy resignation. Into thy loving hands I commend my spirit. Thy blessed will be done, whether by life or death. Only, O Lord, I beseech thee, forgive all my sins and prepare my soul, by unfeigned faith and true repentance, for the time of my departure, that I may die the death of the righteous, and my last end be his. Wean my heart from the world and all its vanities. Fix it upon the things above which are at thy right hand. Bring the invisible realities of eternity so near that by faith I may have a foretaste of them, as joys substantial and sincere. May the fear of dying be swallowed up by the assured hope of life everlasting. In all my pains of body and anxieties of spirit, may thy consolations refresh and delight my soul. May thy Spirit calm my mind and soothe its sorrows. Be thou, O Saviour, with me, and let thy rod and staff comfort me. Then shall I be confident, and willing rather to depart than live, knowing that while at home in the body I am absent from the Lord, and that when the earthly house of this tabernacle is dissolved I have a building of God, a house not made with hands, eternal in the heavens, and an inheritance beyond the grave, purchased by Thy precious death for all believers, which is undefiled, and that fadeth not away.

And now, O Lord, who art the Prince of glory, who hast abolished death, and destroyed him that has the power of death, even the Devil; who wast thyself dead and art alive again and livest for evermore; fulfil these my desires and petitions, and unto thee, the King eternal, immortal, and invisible, the only wise God and our Saviour, Jesus Christ, I will ascribe the glory of my salvation both now and for evermore. Amen.

Our Father, who art in heaven, etc.

The grace of our Lord Jesus Christ, etc.

No. V.

On Recovery from Sickness.

MOST merciful and gracious God, thou art good, and thou doest good, and thy tender mercies are over all thy works. What I have learned by the hearing of the ear thou hast now taught me by my own happy experience. I was brought low, even to the mouth of the grave; my heart and my flesh failed me, and I said, I shall not live, but die. But thou, O Lord, hast kept me alive that I should not go down into the pit. Thou hast lifted me up from the gates of death, and spared me to recover strength before I go hence and be no more. It is of the Lord's mercies that I have not been cut off in the midst of my days, and while unprepared to die. Bless the Lord, O my soul, and let all that is within me bless his holy name, who has healed my disease and restored my soul, and renewed my youth, health, and vigor. O Lord, I would praise thee for thy goodness and for thy mercy, which endureth for ever. Thou hast remembered me in my low estate; thou hast heard my prayer; thou hast had pitiful compassion upon thy most unworthy servant, so that he shall not die, but live, and declare the works of the Lord. The living, the living in the midst of the dying, O may I live to love, and serve, and praise Thee. O may I love Thee more and serve thee better every day.

O Lord, who hast heard the voice of my supplication and delivered my soul from death, what shall I render unto thee for all this unmerited mercy shown unto me? May

I walk before thee in the land of the living; may I take the cup of salvation, and pay unto thee the vows my soul in anguish made. I will offer unto thee in the presence of thy people the sacrifices of thanksgiving, and call upon thy name; I will present body, soul, and spirit unto thee, whose mercies crown my days, as my most reasonable service; I will live not unto myself, or as if I were mine own, but unto Him who so loved me as to give himself for me; who bought me with the price of his own precious blood, and in whom I now live and have my being.

O thou God of grace, give me grace that the life thy goodness has preserved may be thus unreservedly dedicated to thee. May I not live to spend my strength in the pursuit of worldly vanity, or in heaping up riches, or in selfish ease, sinful ungodliness, and unbelief. May I not live to abuse thy long suffering and forbearing mercy. O Lord, have compassion upon me, and grant me thy Holy Spirit to work in me to will and to do according to thy good pleasure; so that the life spared may be spent in holiness and righteousness toward Thee, and in serving my generation in the promotion of the temporal and spiritual welfare of my fellow-men, according to the will of God. O keep me by thy power, merciful Saviour, lest I sin, and some worse thing come upon me. Dispose my heart, and help me to give all diligence to make my calling and election sure, and to work out my salvation with fear and trembling. Make me always mindful how frail I am; how helpless; how easily prostrated and brought low; how soon I may die, and how certainly I must die; and how surely I must stand after death before the judgment seat of Christ to receive according to the deeds done in my body, whether they have been good or evil; and may I, therefore, be enabled so to live as that every day shall be a step nearer to the fruition of thine everlasting glory. Grant this, O most merciful Father, for Christ's sake, my only Mediator and Redeemer. Amen.

Our Father, who art in heaven, etc.

The grace of our Lord Jesus Christ, etc.

SHORT PRAYERS.

For Morning.

MERCIFUL God and Father, I have both laid me down and slept in peace and have awaked in health, because thou, O Lord, hast sustained me. Bless the Lord, O my soul, for these mercies, and for every other good and perfect gift that comes down from Him. As thou preserved me from all the dangers of the night, may thy powerful providence sustain and succor me through this day from danger, disease, and death. Pardon my sins, and convert my soul, and grant me thy salvation. May I spend this day in thy fear, as seeing Thee who art not far from any one of us, and be kept by thy grace from all temptation. May I be attentive to every duty, and watchful against anger, evil speaking, and the sins that most easily beset me. May I be contented, cheerful, and happy, whatever may happen, and be alike prepared for peace or war, for life or death.

Our Father, who art in heaven, etc.

The grace of our Lord and Saviour Jesus

Christ, and the love of God, and the communion of the Holy Ghost, be with my soul. Amen.

> This day I wake me up from sleep,
> I pray thee, Lord. my soul to keep;
> If I should die before it close,
> With thee in bliss may I repose;
> And this I beg for thy Name's sake.

For Evening.

AT the close of another day I come unto thee, O Lord, who art the good Shepherd who never slumbers, nor sleeps, and commit into thy hands my body, soul, and spirit. Thou art my creator, preserver, and most gracious Redeemer, who hast bought me with thy most precious blood. O receive me into thy kingdom of grace now, and into thy kingdom of glory hereafter. Speak peace to my soul. Give me power to repent and believe, and hope in thy power and willingness to save my soul. May I rest peacefully under the shadow of thy wings, and enjoy refreshing sleep, undisturbed by any sudden alarm of raging foes. Grant these blessings also to my comrades in arms, and preserve us all from painful disease and unprepared death. May I awake in the morning in health and strength, fitted for the duties and dangers of the day. Bless all my dear friends, and may we be spared to meet again in peace and prosperity, to rejoice before thee all the days of our lives. Grant these requests, O God, for Christ's sake, in whose words I would further call upon thee as

Our Father, who art in heaven, etc.

The grace of our Lord and Saviour Jesus Christ, etc.

> This night I lay me down to sleep,
> I pray thee, Lord, my soul to keep;
> If I should die before I wake,
> I pray thee, Lord, my soul to take;
> And this I beg for thy Name's sake.

On Going into Battle.

O LORD, into thine hands I commit my spirit, for thou hast redeemed me, O Lord God of truth. With thee are the issues of life and death. Thou hast the keys of death and the grave, so that when thou openest no man shutteth, and when thou shuttest no man can open. All events are at thy command. I leave myself entirely at thy disposal in this battle, not knowing what shall befall me, whether life or death. Prepare me, O gracious Father, to live or to die; so that, whether living or dying, I may be the Lord's. May a sense of pardoned sin and peace with thee through our Lord and Saviour Jesus Christ cast out all fear, and enable me, as a good and faithful soldier, to fight manfully, and contend earnestly against the enemies of my beloved country, and in defence of life and liberty, of our mothers, wives, and sisters, of our homes and happiness, and of a pure Bible, and a freedom to serve and worship God according to its teachings and the dictates of conscience. Righteous Father, vindicate the oppressed, and avenge us of our adversaries. If I perish, may our cause triumph. Take my family and friends into thy divine keeping, and save my soul, and receive me into thy glory, O Lord, through Jesus Christ, my Lord and Saviour. Amen.

In Prospect of Battle.

O LORD God, from whom I have received life, and by whom that life has been preserved until this present moment, I would humbly and confidently commit myself to thy holy keeping in the prospect of coming battle. May thoughts suitable to so solemn an occasion take possession of my mind, and in the fear of the Lord may I go onward. Believing that the cause in which I am engaged is just and righteous, and in defence of the sacred rights, honor, liberty, and independence of our beloved country, and for the truth of thy Word, the honor of thy Name, and the glory of thy holy, wise, and powerful providence, I would desire to feel the courage and determination of a loyal, patriotic, and faithful soldier, and to perform my duty faithfully. Thou art my almighty shield, and canst ward off danger in the midst of the conflict. If it be thy holy will, may my life be preserved while I remain steadfast to my post, and let all cowardly fear be banished from my heart. May I feel safe under thy providence, and may I trust thee for life or for death. Grant that my soul may be redeemed by the blood of Christ, and should it be thy purpose that I should fall, may the sting of death, which is sin, be taken away. May the shield of thy protection be placed before my comrades, and may they all cast themselves on thy mercy. O Lord, grant that victory may rest on our banners, and discomfit our enemies, who wage wicked and cruel war against us. May

God pardon their sins- and save their souls, but destroy their lives, and deliver us from them, and give us victory over them. To thee, O Lord, I now commit my soul and body, and may I not forget thee amid the roar of battle. This I earnestly ask for Christ's sake; and to the Father, Son, and Holy Ghost shall be all the praise. Amen.

On Sentinel and Picket Duty.

OH GOD, who hast brought this war upon us, and made it the duty and privilege of every citizen who is able to come up to the help of our invaded and oppressed country against her wicked and tyrannical enemies, I come to thee for wisdom, power, and protection. I am commanded to occupy the outpost of danger, and to protect our army from sudden surprise. Go with me, and may thy gracious presence cheer and support me. Help me to be sober, vigilant, faithful, and fearless, and use well my eyes and ears in detecting danger and announcing its approach. Preserve me from being overcome by sleep, or betrayed by carelessness, or destroyed by presumption. Deliver me from the deceitful foe, and from the unseen danger.

Teach me how to improve the time by calling upon thee in prayer, meditating on thy glorious gospel, and holding communion with a reconciled God, Father, and Friend, a gracious Redeemer, and a most gracious Comforter. And do thou, O God, search me, and try my heart, and discover to me every evil way that is in me, and lead me in the way everlasting. Grant, O God, these mercies for the sake and merits of thy Son, our blessed Saviour and Redeemer. Amen.

When Sick and Wounded.

O MOST righteous God, thou hast seen fit to lay me aside from active duty, and to appoint for me pain and suffering; may I patiently submit to thy holy will, and be kept from murmuring and repining. Thou canst heal the maladies of my body, and make the remedies employed efficacious. If it be for thy glory, may I be restored to health, and may I yet live to serve my God and my country. Grant, too, that I may be prepared for all that may happen, so that whether I live I may live to the Lord, or whether I die I may die to the Lord, and living or dying still be his. This I ask for the Saviour's sake. Amen.

For Divine Guidance.

O LORD, thou who art the hearer of prayer, be pleased in thy infinite mercy to fill my heart with thy grace, that I may be safely kept amid all the temptations of camp-life. Surrounded as I am, by many who have not the fear of God before their eyes, and whose conversation and conduct are ungodly, let me not be led away by their example. As thou, Lord, seest me, may I fear to commit any known sin. May I never be led to take thy name in vain, and suffer me not in thoughtlessness or passion to use profane language, for thou wilt not hold him guiltless that taketh thy name in vain. Guard me also from intemperance, by which reason is blinded and the soul unfitted for the presence of God. From every other sin, good Lord, deliver me. When called to the performance of difficult and dangerous duties be thou my great protector. Fill my soul with Thy love and fear; cleanse me from every sin of my life in the blood of Christ; and reconcile me to Thee through his atoning sacrifice, so that I may be ever ready to say, The Lord is my refuge, and my present help in trouble. All which I ask for Jesus Christ's sake. Amen.

A General Thanksgiving.

ALMIGHTY God, Father of all mercies, we, thine unworthy servants, do give thee most humble and hearty thanks for all thy goodness and loving kindness to us, and to all men. We bless thee for our creation, preservation, and all the blessings of this life; but, above all, for thine inestimable love in the redemption of the world by our Lord Jesus Christ, for the means of grace, and for the hope of glory. And, we beseech thee, give us that due sense of all thy mercies, that our hearts may be unfeignedly thankful, and that we may show forth thy praise, not only with our lips, but in our lives; by giving up ourselves to thy service, and by walking before thee in holiness and righteousness all our days; through Jesus Christ our Lord, to whom, with thee and the Holy Ghost, be all honor and glory, world without end. Amen.

Thanksgiving.

O ALMIGHTY God, our heavenly Father, we poor sinners lift up our hearts to thee, to bless and praise thy holy name for all thy manifold and great mercies to these Confederate States, from the first day even until now. O most mighty and gracious good God, thy mercy is over all thy works, but in special manner hath been extended toward us, thy people, whom thou hast so powerfully defended. Thou hast showed us wonderful and terrible things; but thou hast continued to protect and bless us, that we might see how powerful and gracious a God thou art; how able and ready to help those who trust in thee. O God, with deep thankfulness of spirit we worship and adore thee for thy protecting power and grace. Be thou still our God, our guide, and mighty defender. And make us, we beseech thee, truly sensible of thy mercies. And give us hearts always ready to express our thankfulness, not only by words, but also by our lives, in being more obedient to thy holy commandments; that we, whom thou hast saved, may serve thee in holiness and righteousness all the days of our lives; through Jesus Christ our Lord and Saviour. Amen. —*Bishop Davis.*

General Prayer.

O MOST powerful and glorious Lord God, the Lord of Hosts, that rulest and commandest all things, thou sittest on the throne judging right, and, therefore, we make our address to thy divine majesty, that thou wouldst take our cause into thine own hands, and judge between us and our enemies. Our trust is in thy mighty power. Stir up thy strength, O Lord, and come and help us, for thou givest not always the battle to the strong, but canst save by many or by few. O let not our sins cry against us for vengeance, but hear us, thy servants, begging mercy and imploring thy help, and that thou wouldst be a defence unto us against the face of our enemies. We implore thy protection and power against those who have invaded our soil and our homes. We humbly look up unto thee, O Lord, and say that we have done them no wrong. Raise up thy power and come among us, and with great might help us. Be thou our stronghold in the day of our calamity. We flee unto thee for succor, and our hope is in thy great and glorious name. Defend, O Lord, and establish our cause. Endue us with power and strength; give us victory over all our enemies, and make it appear that thou art our Saviour and mighty deliverer, through Jesus Christ our Lord. Amen.—*Bishop Davis.*

Collect.

WE beseech thee, O God, favorably to behold this government and people, now bending before thee in deep humility of heart; confessing their own sins, acknowledging thy divine sovereignty, and earnestly imploring thy heavenly benediction and grace. We are sinful, but thou, O Lord, art holy and merciful. We are weak, but thou art mighty. Draw near and help us; pardon our sins and receive and answer our prayers. Bless our rulers, direct their counsels, unite their hearts, strengthen their hands, and prosper all their undertakings. And may it please thee, O Lord God, to visit and bless this whole people in this time of danger and trial. Be thou our present helper and defender, and a strong tower against the face of our enemies. Give courage and strength to our army and navy. Fight with us, O God, against those who are threatening our homes, our firesides, and our families. Confound their counsels, bring to naught their wicked devices, subdue their pride, break their power, and deliver us from all their oppressions and wrongs; that we, thy people, being hurt by no persecutions, may be preserved evermore to glorify thee. who art the only giver of all victory. Grant this, O Father Almighty, for the sake of thy blessed Son, our Redeemer and Saviour Jesus Christ. Amen.—*Bishop Davis.*

Confession.

ALMIGHTY and most merciful Father, we have erred, and strayed from thy ways like lost sheep. We have followed too much the devices and desires of our own hearts. We have offended against thy holy laws. We have left undone those things which we ought to have done, and we have done those things which we ought not to have done, and there is no health in us. But thou, O Lord, have mercy upon us, miserable offenders. Spare thou those, O God, who confess their faults. Restore thou those who are penitent, according to thy promises declared unto mankind, in Christ Jesus our Lord. And grant, O merciful Father, for his sake, that we may hereafter live a godly, righteous, and sober life, to the glory of thy holy name. Amen.

For Defence.

O GOD, who art the author of peace and lover of concord, in knowledge of whom standeth our eternal life, whose service is perfect freedom; defend us, thy humble servants, in all assaults of our enemies; that we, surely trusting in thy defence, may not fear the power of any adversaries, through the might of Jesus Christ our Lord. Amen.

A Prayer for Soldiers under Sentence of Death.

O FATHER of mercies, and God of all comfort, we fly unto thee for succor in behalf of these thy servants, who are now under the sentence of condemnation. The day of their calamity is at hand, and they are accounted as of those who go down into the pit. Blessed Lord, remember thy mercies; look upon their infirmities; hear the voice of their complaint; give them, we beseech thee, patience in this their time of adversity, and support under the terrors which encompass them; set before their eyes the things they have done in the body, which have justly provoked thee to anger; and forasmuch as their continuance appeareth to be short among us, quicken them so much the more by thy grace and Holy Spirit; that they, being converted and reconciled to thee, before thy judgments have cut them off from the earth, may at the hour of their death depart in peace, and be received into thy everlasting kingdom, through Jesus Christ our Lord. Amen.

For Forgiveness.

ALMIGHTY and everlasting God, who hatest nothing that thou hast made, and dost forgive the sins of all those who are penitent, create and make in us new and contrite hearts, that we, worthily lamenting our sins and acknowledging our wretchedness, may obtain of thee, the God of all mercy, perfect remission and forgiveness, through Jesus Christ our Lord. Amen.

For Direction.

DIRECT us, O Lord, in all our doings, with thy most gracious favor, and further us with thy continual help; that in all our works begun, continued, and ended in thee, we may glorify thy holy name, and finally, by thy mercy, obtain everlasting life; through Jesus Christ our Lord. Amen.

On Deliverance from Enemies.

O ALMIGHTY God, who art a strong tower of defence unto thy servants against the face of their enemies, we yield thee praise and thanksgiving for our deliverance from those great and apparent dangers wherewith we were compassed. We acknowledge it is of thy goodness that we were not delivered over as a prey unto them; and beseech thee still to continue such thy mercies toward us, that all the world may know that thou art our Saviour and mighty Deliverer; through Jesus Christ our Lord. Amen.

Prayer for those Exposed to Danger.

ALMIGHTY God, the Saviour of all men, we humbly ask thy tender care and sure protection for thy servants who have come forth at the call of their country, to defend its government and to protect its people in their property and homes, their rights and liberties, their wives and children, their sisters and servants, their altars and their Bibles. Let thy fatherly hand, we beseech thee, be over us; let thy Holy Spirit be with us; let thy good angels have charge of us; with thy loving kindness defend us as with a shield, and either bring us out of our peril in safety, with a heart to show forth thy praises for ever, or else sustain us with that glorious hope, by which alone thy servants can have victory in suffering and death; through the sole merits of Jesus Christ our Lord. Amen.

Prayer during our present National Troubles.

O ALMIGHTY God, who art a strong tower of defence to those who put their trust in Thee, whose power no creature is able to resist, we make our humble cry to thee in this hour of our country's need. Thy property is always to have mercy. Deal not with us according to our sins, neither reward us according to our iniquities; but stretch forth the right hand of thy majesty, and be our defence for thy Name's sake. Shed upon the counsels of our rulers the spirit of wisdom, and moderation, and firmness, and unite the hearts of our people as the heart of one man in upholding the supremacy of law, and the cause of justice and peace, and the sacred rights, honor, and independence of our Confederacy. Abate the violence of passion; banish pride and prejudice from every heart; turn away ungodliness from us, and incline us all to trust in thy righteous providence, and to be ready for every duty, enduring hardship as good soldiers, and bearing patiently every needful sacrifice and self-denial. And oh, that in thy great mercy thou wouldst make this war to cease, and so order all things that peace and happiness, truth and justice, religion and piety, may be established among us for all generations. These things, and whatever else thou shalt see to be necessary and convenient for us, we humbly beg through the merits and mediation of Jesus Christ our Lord and Saviour. Amen.

To be used in Ships of War.

O ETERNAL Lord God, who alone spreadest out the heavens, and rulest the raging of the sea; who hast compassed the waters with bounds, until day and night come to an end; be pleased to receive into thy Almighty and most gracious protection the persons of us thy servants, and the fleet [*or ship*] in which we serve. Preserve us from the dangers of the sea, and from the violence of the enemy; that we may be a safeguard unto the Confederate States of America, and a security for such as pass on the seas upon their lawful occasions; that the inhabitants of our land may in peace and quietness serve thee our God; and that we may return in safety to enjoy the blessings of the land, with the fruits of our labor; and, with a thankful remembrance of thy mercies, to praise and glorify thy holy name, through Jesus Christ our Lord. Amen.

Sailors' Prayer.

O GOD our Father! wash us from all our sins in the Saviour's blood, and we shall be whiter than snow. Create in us a clean heart, and fill us with the Holy Ghost, that we may never be ashamed to confess the faith of Christ crucified, and manfully to fight under his banner against sin, the world, and the Devil; looking to Jesus the great Captain of our salvation. We ask it all, because he lived, died, rose again, and ever liveth to make intercession for us. Amen.

During a Storm.

O MOST powerful and glorious Lord God, at whose command the winds blow and lift up the waves of the sea, and who stillest the rage thereof; we, thy creatures, but miserable sinners, do in this our great distress cry unto thee for help: Save, Lord, or else we perish. We confess when we have been safe, and seen all things quiet about us, we have forgotten thee, our God, and refused to hearken to the still voice of thy Word, and to obey thy commandments; but now we see how terrible thou art in all thy works of wonder; the great God to be feared above all; and therefore we adore thy Divine Majesty, acknowledging thy power, and imploring thy goodness. Help, Lord, and save us for thy mercies' sake, in Jesus Christ, thy Son our Lord. Amen.

Thanksgiving After a Storm.

O MOST mighty and gracious good God, thy mercy is over all thy works, but in special manner hath been extended toward us, whom thou hast so powerfully and wonderfully defended. Thou hast showed us terrible things, and wonders in the deep, that we might see how powerful and gracious a God thou art; how able and ready to help those who trust in thee. Thou hast showed us how both winds and seas obey thy commands; that we may learn even from them hereafter to obey thy voice, and to do thy will. We therefore bless and glorify thy name for this thy mercy, in saving us when we were ready to perish. And we beseech thee, make us as truly sensible now of thy mercy as we were then of the danger; and give us hearts always ready to express our thankfulness, not only by words, but also by our lives, in being more obedient to thy holy commandments. Continue, we beseech thee, this thy goodness to us; that we, whom thou hast saved, may serve thee. in holiness and righteousness all the days of our lives, through Jesus Christ our Lord and Saviour. Amen.

For a Sick Person.

O FATHER of mercies and God of all comfort, our only help in time of need, look down from heaven, we humbly beseech thee, behold, visit, and relieve thy sick *ser-*

vant, for whom our prayers are desired. Look upon him with the eyes of thy mercy; comfort him with a sense of thy goodness; preserve him from the temptations of the enemy; give him patience under his affliction; and, in thy good time, restore him to health, and enable him to lead the residue of his life in thy fear and to thy glory. Or else give him grace so to take thy visitation that, after this painful life ended, he may dwell with thee in life everlasting; through Jesus Christ our Lord. Amen.

After Sudden Visitation.

O MOST gracious Father, we fly unto thee for mercy in behalf of this thy servant here lying under the sudden visitation of thine hand. If it be thy will, preserve his life, that there may be place for repentance. But if thou hast otherwise appointed, let thy mercy supply to him the want of the usual opportunity for the trimming of his lamp. Stir up in him such sorrow for sin and such fervent love to thee, as may in a short time do the work of many days. That among the praises which thy saints and holy angels shall sing to the honor of thy mercy through eternal ages, it may be to thy unspeakable glory, that thou hast redeemed the soul of this thy servant from eternal death, and made him partaker of the everlasting life, which is through Jesus Christ our Lord. Amen.

For Close of any Service.

ALMIGHTY God, who hast given us grace at this time with one accord to make our common supplications unto thee, and dost promise that when two or three are gathered together in thy name thou wilt grant their requests, fulfil now, O Lord, the desires and petitions of thy servants, as may be most expedient for them; granting us in this world knowledge of thy truth, and in the world to come life everlasting. Amen.

The Creed.

I BELIEVE in God the Father Almighty, maker of heaven and earth; and in Jesus Christ his only Son, our Lord; who was conceived by the Holy Ghost, born of the Virgin Mary; suffered under Pontius Pilate, was crucified, dead, and buried; he descended into hell:* the third day he rose again from the dead; he ascended into heaven, and sitteth on the right hand of God the Father Almighty; from thence he shall come to judge the quick and the dead. I believe in the Holy Ghost; the Holy Catholic Church; the Communion of Saints; the forgiveness of sins; the resurrection of the body; and the life everlasting. Amen.

Gloria in Excelsis.

GLORY be to God on high, and on earth peace, good will toward men. We praise thee, we bless thee, we worship thee, we glorify thee, we give thanks unto thee for thy great glory, O Lord God, heavenly King, God the Father Almighty.

O Lord, the only begotten Son, Jesus Christ; O Lord God, Lamb of God, Son of the Father, that takest away the sins of the world, have mercy upon us. Thou that takest away the sins of the world, have mercy upon us. Thou that takest away the sins of the world, receive our prayer. Thou that sittest at the right hand of God the Father, have mercy upon us.

---

* i. e. Continued in the state of the dead, and under the power of death, until the third day.

For thou only art holy; thou only art the Lord; thou only, O Christ, with the Holy Ghost, art most high in the glory of God the Father. Amen.

The Ten Commandments.

I. Thou shalt have none other gods but me.

II. Thou shalt not make to thyself any graven image, nor the likeness of anything that is in heaven above, or in the earth beneath, or in the water under the earth. Thou shalt not bow down to them, nor worship them; for I the Lord thy God am a jealous God, and visit the sins of the fathers upon the children unto the third and fourth generation of them that hate me; and show mercy unto thousands in them that love me and keep my commandments.

III. Thou shalt not take the name of the Lord thy God in vain; for the Lord will not hold him guiltless that taketh his name in vain.

IV. Remember that thou keep holy the Sabbath day. Six days shalt thou labor, and do all that thou hast to do; but the seventh day is the Sabbath of the Lord thy God; in it thou shalt do no manner of work, thou, and thy son, and thy daughter, thy man servant, and thy maid servant, thy cattle, and the stranger that is within thy gates. For in six days the Lord made heaven and earth, the sea, and all that in them is, and rested the seventh day. Wherefore the Lord blessed the seventh day, and hallowed it.

V. Honor thy father and thy mother, that thy days may be long in the land which the Lord thy God giveth thee.

VI. Thou shalt do no murder.

VII. Thou shalt not commit adultery.

VIII. Thou shalt not steal.

IX. Thou shalt not bear false witness against thy neighbor.

X. Thou shalt not covet thy neighbor's house; thou shalt not covet thy neighbor's wife, nor his servant, nor his maid, nor his ox, nor his ass, nor anything that is his.

O Lord, have mercy upon us, and incline our hearts to keep these laws, for Christ's sake. Amen.

Come unto me all ye that labor and are heavy laden, and I will give you rest. Take my yoke upon you, and learn of me, for I am meek and lowly in heart, and ye shall find rest for your souls; for my yoke is easy, and my burden is light.—MATT. xi, 28, 29, 30.

For God so loved the world that he gave his only begotten Son, that whosoever believeth in him should not perish, but have everlasting life.—JOHN iii, 16.

This is a true saying, and worthy of all acceptation, that Christ Jesus came into the world to save sinners, of whom I am Chief. —1 TIM. i, 15.

If any man sin we have an advocate with the Father, Jesus Christ, the righteous; and he is the propitiation for our sins.—1 JOHN ii, 1, 2.

SELECTIONS OF SCRIPTURE FOR USE ON VARIOUS OCCASIONS.

For a Day of Thanksgiving.

Exod. ch. 3, 14, 15, 17.
Deut. ch. 7, 28, 35.
Josh. ch. 4.
2 Sam. ch. 7.
1 Kings, ch. 12.
1 Chron. ch. 16, 17, v. 16–27.
2 Chron. ch. 7, 30, 31.
Ezra, ch. 7.
Nehem. ch. 8, 12.
Ps. 18, 20, 31, 33, 34, 46, 47, 48, 66, 68, 75, 76, 77, 78, 85, 89, 96, 97, 98, 105, 106, 107, 108, 110, 117, 118, 124, 125, 126, 135, 136, 145, 146, 147.

Esther, ch. 5, 7, 8, 9. Is. ch. 14, 25, 26, 37, 38.
Lament. ch. 3. 1 Tim. ch. 2.
Ezek. ch. 39. Rev. ch. 4, 5, 6, 7,
Zephan. ch. 3. 15, 18, 19.

For a Day of Humiliation.

Gen. ch. 18, 32. 60, 62, 63, 64, 69,
Exod. ch. 32, 33. 70, 71, 74, 78, 79,
Numb. ch. 13, 14. 80, 81, 82, 86, 90,
Deut. ch. 4, 9, 10, 11, 91, 94, 102; 115,
  27, 28, 29, 30, 32. 123, 137, 140, 144.
Judges, ch. 6. Is. ch. 1, 3, 5, 7, 8,
2 Sam. ch. 24. 10, 13, 22, 24, 33,
1 Kings, ch. 8, 18, 21. 34, 36, 37; 44, v.
2 Kings, ch. 17, 18, 1–8 and v. 21–28;
  19, 20, 23, 24, 25. 59, 63, 64.
1 Chron. ch. 21. Jer. ch. 2, 5, 6, 7, 8,
2 Chron. ch. 6, 30, 9, 11, 13, 14, 16,
  34, 35. 17, 18, 19, 20, 21,
Ezra, ch. 8, 9, 10. 22, 42, 46.
Nehem. 1, 2, 4, 6, 9, Sam. ch. 1, 4, 5.
  10, 13. Ezek. 6, 11, 14, 18,
Esther, ch. 3, 4. 21, 22, 25, 33, 34,
Job, ch. 1, 40, 41. 36.
Ps. 2, 7, 9, 10, 11, 17, Dan. ch. 3, 4, 5, 6, 9.
  22, 27, 28, 35, 37, Hos. ch. 7, 14.
  38, 41, 42, 43, 44, Joel, ch. 1, 2, 3.
  52, 55, 56, 57, 59, Amos, ch. 5.

SELECTIONS OF SCRIPTURE. 151

Obad.
Jonah, ch. 3, 12.
Micah, ch. 6.
Habak. ch. 3.
Zech. ch. 9.
Mal. ch. 1, 3.
Matt. ch. 5, 6, 7, 8, 14, 18, 24, 25.

Luke, ch. 13.
Acts, 4, 5, 12, 16, 27.
Rom. ch. 13.
2 Cor. ch. 1.
1 Pet. ch. 1, 2, 4.
2 Pet. ch. 2, 3.
Jude.
Rev. ch. 2, 3.

For Victory.

Gen. ch. 14.
Numb. ch. 21.
Deut. c. 7, 28, v. 1–14.
Deut. ch. 31, v. 1–8.
Josh. ch. 8, 10, 11, 33.
Judges, 4, 5, 7, 20.
1 Sam. ch. 7, 14, 17, 30.
2 Sam. ch. 5, 8, 10, 18, 22.

1 Kings, ch. 20.
2 Kings, ch. 3.
1 Chron. ch. 19.
2 Chron. ch. 20, 32.
Ps. 9, 18, 21, 31, 44, 46, 47, 48, 76, 77, 78, 124, 135; and many of those under Thanksgiving.
Josh. 23, 24.

For Repulse.

Josh. ch. 7.
2 Chron. ch. 18.
Is. ch. 30, 42; and several under Humiliation.
Gen. ch. 49, v. 28–33, and ch. 50, v. 1–14.

Jer. ch. 46, 50.
Deut. ch. 84.
Josh. ch. 23, and 24 in part.
Judges, ch. 16.
1 Sam. ch. 2, v. 1–11.
1 Sam. ch. 4.

152   SELECTIONS OF SCRIPTURE.

1 Sam. ch. 18, v. 1–4.
1 Sam. ch. 20 in part, and 2 Sam. ch 1.
1 Sam. ch. 31, and 2 Sam. ch. 1, v. 25–27.
2 Sam. ch. 18.
Job, ch. 7, 14.
Ps. 39, 44, 49, 60, 78, 79, 90, 103.

Eccles. ch. 9, v. 1–5, v. 10, and ch. 11 and 12.
Is. 28, 38, 40, v. 1–11, and v. 26–31; 57, v. 1–3.
Rom. ch. 5.
1 Cor. ch. 15.
2 Cor. ch. 4, 5.
1 Thess. ch. 4.

For Funerals.

1 Tim. ch. 6, v. 6–21.
2 Tim. ch. 4, v. 1–17, and v. 19–22.
Heb. ch. 11, 12.
James, ch. 5.
1 Pet. ch. 1.

2 Pet. ch. 1, 3.
1 John, ch. 2, 3, 5.
Rev. ch. 4, 5, 6, part of each; 7, 15, 20, 21, 22, or parts of.

For Peace.

Ps. 29, 30, 44, 46, 47, 53, 54, 57, 58, 59, 65, 68, 85, 89, 97, 98, 105, 106, 111, 114, 116, 122, 126, 127, 136, 144, 147.
Is. ch. 11, 12, 25, 26, 32, 35, 51, 52, 54, 61, 62, 65, v. 17–25.

Jer. ch. 30, 31, 32, 33, v. 36–44.
Ezek. ch. 37, v. 1–13.
Nahum, ch. 1.
Zeph. ch. 3.
Zech. ch. 8, 14.
Luke, ch. 1, v. 46–56, and v. 67–80.

www.ingramcontent.com/pod-product-compliance
Lightning Source LLC
Chambersburg PA
CBHW030341170426
43202CB00010B/1194